# PRAISE FOR *LOVE AT FIRST FIGHT*

"*Love at First Fight* is a delight! My husband and I read parts of it together, and we both laughed out loud at Dena and Carey's first-person narratives. Having enjoyed our own marital adventure for thirty-seven years, we could well relate to the different issues and discoveries that the authors share from their own marriage; the prayers, advice, and questions to consider all rang true and offer a valuable resource to any married couple who want to make their marriage relationship the best it can possibly be."

—Jan Dunlap, author of the international bestseller *Saved by Gracie: How a Rough-and-Tumble Rescue Dog Dragged Me Back to Health, Happiness, and God* (Authentic Publishers, 2014)

"Approaching the seriousness of marriage in a lighthearted manner, Carey and Dena Dyer help couples laugh through the tears, accept each other's flaws, and love each other through it all. Complete with tips from marriage pros and thought-provoking discussion questions, Carey and Dena demonstrate that every couple can hit a home run in their marriage, even if they experience a few strikes along the way."

—Michelle Lazurek, author of *An Invitation to the Table*

"We can sometimes feel alone in the issues that we encounter in our marriages. Hearing from those who are a little further down the road can be helpful. In *Love at First Fight*, Dena and Carey Dyer share the inside story of their marriage with humor and transparency, allowing readers a deeper look into their own marriages. Within each devotion is a section titled *He Says* or *She Says*, providing the male and female perspective of marriage—making this book perfect for couples to share. Each devotion ends with advice from a seasoned married couple underscoring the message and adding wisdom to the stories. *Love at First Fight* fills a need for couples who want to understand each other and deepen the intimacy of their marriage. Reading this book together can facilitate conversations to help a couple grow closer."

—Betsy Duffey, author, *The Shepherd's Song* and *The Lord Is Their Shepherd: Praying Psalm 23 for Your Children*

"A devotional that is creative, fabulous, and funny all rolled into one! I love the format of this book. *Love at First Fight* is a unique approach to helping couples learn about and laugh at the characteristic differences between men and women. Fresh, insightful, deep, and distinctive, the Dyers have captured it all."

—Laura Petherbridge, speaker and author of *When "I Do" Becomes "I Don't," The Smart Stepmom*, and *101 Tips for the Smart Stepmom*

"Carey and Dena Dyer share their ups and downs in marriage—universal ups and downs. They are open and honest about themselves and their marriage. This is not a book about the perfect marriage; it's about a real marriage. It is insightful, funny, and thought-provoking. *Love at First Fight* is for engaged couples, newlyweds, and couples married fifty years."

—Susan K. Stewart, founder of PracticalInspirations.com and author
of *Formatting e-Books for Writers*

"I laughed out loud, I choked back tears, and I squirmed (recognizing myself) in these wonderful devotional stories by Carey and Dena Dyer. They speak directly to the reality of marriage—the joy, the pain, the learning, the growth, the coming together of two people into one. Marriage is a lifetime adventure, and Carey and Dena testify to the commitment, the care, and the love that make the adventure possible."

—Glynn Young, author of the novels *Dancing Priest* and
*A Light Shining* and the nonfiction book *Poetry at Work*

"In a world of first-person shooters, zero-sum politics, and smartphone dating, we are in desperate need of models for healthy conflict. Dena and Carey share shamelessly from their personal history—everything from the petty war stories to deeper struggles with unemployment and panic attacks. Their practical and inspirational book will teach you and your significant other to always look on the bright side of a fight."

—Marcus Goodyear, author, *Barbies at Communion*

"We recommend *Love at First Fight* for every couple who wants to grow closer to God and each other. No matter how long you've been married or the nature of your marriage history, this book will transform your relationship as you engage in the insightful stories and discussion questions. Put on the gloves of love and learn tangible tips from the marriages of others, including the authors."

—Clint and Penny A. Bragg, authors of *Marriage on the Mend—
Healing Your Relationship After Crisis, Separation, and Divorce*

"Real, honest, funny, and fun. This devotional looks at the differences between men and women and the little things we argue about. It includes his point of view and hers…with stories from their lives. The questions for couples are an excellent ways to start a conversation with your spouse and learn about each other without arguing. This practical book would be fun to talk about on a date, read as an evening devotion, or share it with your spouse as you make a cross-country trip. I highly recommend *Love at First Fight* to strengthen marriages and avoid some of the conflicts couples often face.

—Joyce Zook, author, *12 Keys for Marriage Success*,
PracticalChristianWoman.com

"Research suggests that we are more open to learn new concepts (and even retain them better) when we are having a good time. And a good time will be had by all with Carey and Dena Dyer's new devotional *Love at First Fight*. Transparency is funny—when someone else does it. And the Dyers' willingness to come clean with the conflict they've experienced will bring you a smile of 'been there, done that, too.' The questions at the end of each short chapter will prompt great discussion with you and your honey. And the 'Tips from the Pros' close out each topic with a bit of sage advance from couples who've successfully lived to tell the tale. Don't miss this terrific book!"

—Deb DeArmond, author of *Don't Go to Bed Angry. Stay Up and Fight!* and *I Choose You Today: 31 Choices to Make Love Last*,
Speaker and Coach. debdearmond.com.

"I wish I had read *Love at First Fight* by Carey and Dena Dyer when I was married 55 years ago. I like the honesty of the authors ("…we've learned the most from the failures we've experienced," and "Who knew that marriage would require a million little adjustments every time we were together?"); the humor ("If marriage is a font, then ours is Wingdings"); and the way each chapter is divided into *He Says*, *She Says*, questions: Taking Off the Gloves, and quotations from others: Tips from the Pros. The scriptures used are especially appropriate for each section. You'll want to buy one for yourself and several for gifts."

—Donna Clark Goodrich, author and speaker, www.thewritersfriend.net

# LOVE
# AT FIRST
# FIGHT

52 STORY-BASED MEDITATIONS

FOR MARRIED COUPLES

## CAREY & DENA DYER

**SHILOH RUN** ◢ PRESS
An Imprint of Barbour Publishing, Inc.

# DEDICATION

To our parents.
Thank you for showing us the way.

# CONTENTS

# INTRODUCTION

If marriage is a font, then ours is Wingdings. We've tried being something more respectable, like Times New Roman or Courier, but alas, some couples are destined for weirdness.

Before you picture us as the Addams Family, let me assure you that we have a happy, loving marriage. We've had our fair share of ups and downs, as you'll see, but whatever the circumstances, we've always tried to keep laughter and enjoying each other as priorities.

In our respective careers, we each travel a bit to speak and sing at various churches and events. This book was born out of a desire to work on something together—something that would convey our belief in Christ as the best foundation for a home. We also wanted to share our philosophy that fun is a key ingredient in keeping things from going sour.

So, *humor* and *devotional*—can those two words live together in peace and harmony? We sure hope so!

While this book can be enjoyed alone, our goal is to provide a resource couples can use together. We want you to laugh a little, learn a lot, and maybe even reminisce together about your own story.

By no means do we consider ourselves matrimonial experts; in fact, we've learned the most from the failures we've experienced. Perhaps you can learn from us what not to do, and avoid as many marriage misfires as we've had.

The devotionals can be read in any order, but we've organized them according to the years we've been married. We tell stories from our marriage, not to hold ourselves up as people who have it all together, but to portray realistically the journey we've taken.

As you read through the book, you may notice that the pieces gradually get more serious as we both realized the requirements for a fulfilling life together. Like many couples, we started out naive and progressed to frustrated. Next, we took a detour to discouragement and disillusionment. After a period of true despondency, in which we despaired of making it through together, we found a new level of commitment and joy in our marriage.

For that, we give all thanks and glory to God. We've tried to be honest and vulnerable about both the highs and the lows in order to show the depth of both our mistakes and God's mercy.

We are thankful you picked up *Love at First Fight*, and we pray that it encourages you in whatever stage you're in as a couple. You may be engaged to be married, in the throes of newlywed bliss, or in the middle of midlife malaise. Wherever you are, know that God longs to be the center of your relationship. If you keep Him there, He will do amazing things in and through you.

Did you know that God has brought you two together for a purpose? He has! It's our desire not to just let life happen to us but to be deliberate about our relationship with God and each other.

If you want to do the same, we pray *Love at First Fight* is a helpful tool toward reaching that goal.

# PART 1

# COMING OUT SWINGING

# LOVE ON THE ROAD

*Be completely humble and gentle; be patient, bearing with one another in love.*
*Make every effort to keep the unity of the Spirit through the bond of peace.*
Ephesians 4:2–3

## HE SAYS

The time shortly before we started dating can best be summed up by an old split-panel *Far Side* cartoon. A girl on one side is lying wide awake in bed, saying, "I think he really likes me!" On the other side lies the male object of her affection, who says to himself, "I really like vanilla."

We met in a traveling singing group and spent two years on the road with six other college graduates from all over the United States. Dena, being closely tuned in to God's radar and having unknowingly journaled about me since the age of twelve, saw right off the bat that we would be good together. Still, being the good Christian girl she was raised to be, she never made any advances.

I was just glad to have a close friend on what was, at times, a lonely road trip. For the longest time, I honestly never thought about Dena in "that way." I treated her more like a good-natured dog who would jump up in the truck with you than the delicate, rose-scented love goddess she is.

Our relationship was complicated by the fact that I openly flirted with other girls and talked about them in front of Dena. After all, she was my good buddy, and we could talk about anything:

> Me: Wow, did you see that cute waitress? If we were gonna be in town longer, I'd ask her out! Could you pass the salt?
>
> Dena: (*thinking as she exits to the ladies' room to cry*) *Sure, here's the salt. Why don't you just rub it in my emotional wounds?*

Clueless. Brainless. Whatever you call it, I had a double dip. Finally, thank the good Lord above, I woke up one morning and it was all crystal clear. I didn't just like vanilla; I liked Dena! The feeling gently washed over me like warm sunlight. And it had only taken me a mere ten months longer than her to realize it!

I lovingly expressed my feelings for Dena at a truck stop. (Don't judge. Life on the road doesn't lend itself to private, romantic moments.) My honey should get extra jewels in her crown for not blurting out, "Well, it's about time!"

Yes, I finally came to my senses and arrived at the same place in my heart that she was. Nevertheless, I took the longest possible route and should have stopped somewhere along the way to ask for directions.

## SHE SAYS

Because I had dated a few duds, I knew a catch when I saw one. Carey was the funniest person—but not at others' expense—I'd ever met. He had a passion for the Lord and was crazy about his family and friends. He was terrific with kids. He could also sing like a dream. And—he was darn cute.

It floored me that he didn't see how good we would be together. I could tell he enjoyed my company—after all, we spent most of our free time together. He confided in me his hopes and dreams, and he even talked to me about girls. *Sigh.*

I couldn't figure out how to leave the friend zone. . .and just when I thought I couldn't stand it one more second, he'd burst my bubble.

> Me: (*thinking*) *I have to tell him how I feel. I can't go on like this, hiding my emotions. Surely he knows anyway. Everyone else in the group has figured it out. And isn't it obvious we are destined to be a couple? He needs to father my children.* . . .
>
> Carey: I think it's such a turnoff when a girl makes the first move.

While he was chatting up the ski instructor we met on our day off in Aspen, I left the slopes in tears and found a pay phone (this was in 1994) and called my mom. Again.

"Mom," I gasped through tears. "He doesn't know I'm alive. It's never going to happen!"

"Dena," she said calmly, "we're just going to pray about it."

She prayed, and so did I. And one day Carey started acting differently around me. At first I thought it was just my wishful thinking.

Soon, though, he confessed that he saw me as more than a friend.

Outwardly I said, "I've felt that way for a while," but inwardly I was singing the "Hallelujah Chorus" with the Brooklyn Tabernacle Choir backing me up.

Carey pursued me with the diligence he'd once reserved for trumpet and voice practice—and I enjoyed every single minute of it.

Dear reader, some things are worth waiting for.

*Lord, thank You that Your timing is perfect, even when I think You're taking too long. Help us hold our expectations of You—and our spouses—loosely, trusting Your heart and Your plans for us.*

## TAKING OFF THE GLOVES
- What first attracted you to each other?
- Who made the first move?
- Recreate your first date.

### TIPS FROM THE PROS
*Go on a date once a week. And forget the fifty-fifty advice. When you both feel like you're giving 75 percent, that's probably about right.*
—Elsie and Ronnie Harrel, married 27 years

# LOVE AT FIRST FIGHT

*Starting a quarrel is like breaching a dam;*
*so drop the matter before a dispute breaks out.*
PROVERBS 17:14

## HE SAYS

It was love at first fight. One of the happiest days of our lives also contained our first fuss as a married couple. Dena and I may hold the record for the shortest amount of time between saying "I do" and "Oh no you didn't!"

As we pulled away from the church, wedded bliss became wedded blahs. As was the custom, my groomsmen had decorated our vehicle with an assortment of post-ceremony goodies: shaving cream, cans, and toilet paper. Although I had participated in similar hijinks at many weddings before, I'd never thought about what happens when the car starts moving down the open road. Stuff flies everywhere!

Being the neat freak I am, I wanted to spray off the car at one of those fifty-cent car washes (yes, fifty cents—this was 1995). In retrospect, perhaps I subconsciously wanted to stop and gather my thoughts because I was nervous about. . .well, you know. . .*later* that night.

I am much smarter now than I was then. I've learned the truth of these noble words from the poet Ogden Nash ("A Word to Husbands"):

To keep your marriage brimming
With love in the loving cup,
Whenever you're wrong, admit it;
Whenever you're right, shut up.

## SHE SAYS

When Carey told me he wanted to stop and clean the car, my first thought was, *Are you kidding me? I've been waiting my whole adult life for my wedding night. I've got Elisabeth Elliot's* Passion and Purity *dog-eared and underlined more than my Bible. And he wants to stop and wash the car!*

I was, simply put, exasperated. As a girl who had just floated through her long-awaited dream wedding, I was extremely proud of our blinged-out Buick. The cans, shaving cream, and Charmin streamers told the world, "We're hitched! She—and he—are off the market! No more blind dates, awkward rejections, or singles' mixers. Let the eternal happiness commence!"

Ironic, right?

I reluctantly agreed to let Carey pull over at the nearest car wash, with one caveat: he had to be quick. However, once he started spraying water and pulling items off the car, it seemed he couldn't stop. For the love of Pete, he started *detailing the thing.*

Now I wasn't just flummoxed. I was furious. And Carey was confused. He hadn't a clue what he had done wrong, poor guy.

Thankfully, we had a forty-five-minute drive to our hotel. Along the way, Carey made me laugh so hard that I almost forgot what I was mad about. And when we got to our hotel room—which was on the concierge floor, a huge splurge for us—we decided to make up in the best possible way.

*Father, thank You for the gift of laughter. Thank You, too, for the gift of our spouses. When our polar opposite personalities rub each other the wrong way, help us be quick to forgive. Remind us that those qualities that irritate us are the very ones that attracted us to our mate in the first place. And thank You for the gift of affection, which helps strengthen our relationship.*

## TAKING OFF THE GLOVES

- We've heard it said that weaknesses are just strengths gone too far. How would it help you if you could reframe those things that annoy you and see them as your spouse's strengths?
- If possible, take a personality test together and discuss the results. You'll most likely see things from a different perspective. (Dena says: "When I went through a personality course, I realized that Carey wasn't out to get me—he was just doing things that came naturally. It was incredibly helpful!")
- Look through your wedding album or watch the recording together and reminisce about how young, idealistic—and in love—you were.

## TIPS FROM THE PROS

*Be present for your spouse, physically and emotionally. Choose your battles. Live with each other's idiosyncrasies. Laugh at yourself.*

—Bill and Judy Vriesema, married 33 years

# SOUR GRAPES AND
# THROWN TOMATOES

*House and land are handed down from parents,*
*but a congenial spouse comes straight from GOD.*
PROVERBS 19:14 MSG

## HE SAYS

The tiny kitchen in our first apartment was the stage for our second heated discussion. The ink was still drying on our marriage license, and Dena brought home our very first load of groceries. As we (translation: *she*) began to stock the fridge with the best food coupons could buy, I noticed that her "method" for organizing the food in the refrigerator was different than mine—that is, she didn't *have* a method. There was no rhyme or reason to what food went where. (I mean, they label those drawers and bins for a reason, right? The names are there to help you!)

At this point, I want to point out a pattern you may have noticed by now. Several of the disagreements early in our marriage stemmed from Dena's lack of attention to detail and my borderline OCD overattention to detail.

That should give you a little more context to what I said next. As poor, innocent Dena randomly dumped groceries into the refrigerator, giving no consideration to container dimensions (doesn't everyone put the liquid jugs in shortest to tallest?), I thought that the loving, caring thing to do was to give her a piece of friendly advice. "Honey," I said, "thanks so much for getting the groceries. But when it comes to putting them away, I think you might benefit from an orderly system I learned from my mother."

It's a good thing there wasn't an iron skillet in our almost-kitchen, or I'd have been seeing stars. Take my advice, men: in the name of hospital emergency rooms everywhere, *never* invoke the name of your mother for at least the first year of marriage.

Don't get me wrong; my mom is a wonderful person, and Dena loves her very much. However, new brides are usually insecure about "measuring up" to the matriarch of their hubby's family. Hindsight is twenty-twenty. I definitely should have held my OCD tongue on that occasion, spared my wife's feelings, and gone on to other detail-oriented pursuits, like counting the exact number of stairs leading away from our apartment.

## SHE SAYS

I was infuriated when Carey mentioned how my mother-in-law liked the fridge arranged. After an hour of coupon clipping and two hours of shopping (in the Texas heat, no less), being oh-so-careful with our minuscule grocery budget, I think my exact words to him were, "If *you* want to go get the groceries, *you* can arrange them any way you want." As they're wont to do, my nostrils flared when I said it. And my face turned as red as the tomatoes I'd bought on clearance.

Carey's mom cooks like a chef and keeps a spotless house, no matter what, and it's hard not to compare myself to her (even after twenty years). Not that she would ever make me feel bad; she's as sweet as they come. Believe me, I can give myself a guilt trip all on my own.

Thankfully, I have learned over these past two decades to revel in my gifts instead of comparing myself to other moms and wives. After all, there will always be someone who is thinner, prettier, richer, a better cook/writer/ etc., than me. However, God has lovingly reminded me—over and over— that He created me just as I am. He placed me in the position of Carey's wife (and Jordan and Jackson's mom) in His perfect providence.

When I rest in that, I'm much less likely to throw those tomatoes at Carey.

*God, give us the grace to see each other's gifts instead of our limitations.*
*Help us think before we speak and be patient with one another*
*when our differences clash. We love You, Lord, and we want to*
*love each other well. Give us Your mercy as we seek to do so.*

## TAKING OFF THE GLOVES

- In what areas do you feel insecure? How could these insecurities be affecting your marriage?
- Encourage each other today in areas where you excel.
- Have you unfairly criticized your spouse lately? If so, humble yourself and apologize.

## TIPS FROM THE PROS

*Be the type of person you want to be around. Imagine walking in the front door*
*after a hard day and receiving the kind of welcome you'd most like. Then give it.*
—ANITA BROOKS, MARRIED 37 YEARS

# MY LONE STAR SWEETHEART

*Trust GOD from the bottom of your heart; don't try to figure out everything on your own. Listen for GOD's voice in everything you do, everywhere you go; he's the one who will keep you on track. Don't assume that you know it all.*
PROVERBS 3:5–7 MSG

## HE SAYS

"Wow. Just. . .wow."

That's pretty much what I thought the first time I laid eyes on the love of my life. Of course, I didn't *know* that she was the love of my life. And my exclamation wasn't like, "Wow, I've just seen the bearer of my children." It was more like, "Wow, do they really dress like that in Texas?"

Dena and I first met when we both auditioned for a touring musical group in Atlanta, Georgia. We hailed from different parts of the country. My Tennessee upbringing made me just about as country as corn bread, but even I wasn't prepared for the "Ding Dong Dolly from Dumas, Texas," who stood before me.

For whatever reason, that particular day Dena decided to wear a dress covered in a print featuring colorful cowboy boots. Her ruby-red lipstick topped it all off, as if she were just waiting to follow up a "Howdy!" with a ruby-red kiss on my cheek.

I mean, Dena *did* look cute—she can't help but look cute, even if she were wearing a burlap sack—but *really*? Her dress looked like she was representing Texas in the new "obsessed with my home state" portion of the Miss America pageant.

I guess first impressions can be deceiving at times, because I fell head-over-boots for that little Texas gal. . .and evidently, she doesn't mind corn bread.

## SHE SAYS

When I first met Carey, I remember him acting overfriendly, like a puppy dog. I thought, *Back off, buster! I'm not looking to find a man. I just want to serve God and be a part of this singing group.* He was gregarious and friendly then, and he still is after twenty years. I didn't know he was being nice; I thought he was flirting. And it's funny—I almost never dressed in Western clothes, and I can't remember why I chose to embrace my Texas roots so thoroughly that day.

First impressions can definitely be wrong, and quick assumptions are often faulty. In our marriage, we've learned to question assumptions about the other person. For instance:

- Is he acting rude and/or angry? A wise counselor once told me that all anger is rooted in fear. Instead of taking things personally, pray for God to give you wisdom and patience. When your mate cools off, gently ask him if there is anything he needs to talk about.
- Is she crying and/or being snippy? Instead of assuming it's just hormones and you'll never understand her, pray and ask God for discernment. In a less stressful moment, offer to listen and support her without giving quick fixes.

It takes humility to try and understand our spouses, but this relationship, above all others, is worth the effort we put into it.

*Our Great Provider, thank You for allowing us to meet and fall in love. Forgive us when we assume things or jump to conclusions. Help us to come toward each other with hearts full of humility, gratitude, and unselfishness.*

## TAKING OFF THE GLOVES

- Talk about your first impressions of each other. Were they positive or negative? How did your assumptions change?
- Honestly assess whether either of you is still making assumptions in a specific area of marriage (sex, money, work). As our relationships change, so do our needs and desires.
- Just for fun, look back at old pictures of the two of you. If you're brave, post some on social media.

### TIPS FROM THE PROS

*I never would have thought it could happen, but the older we get, the more madly in love I am with my husband! Just be honest, communicate, and share in all things. Simply said, I am married to my best friend, and we plan to grow older and grayer together.*
—DALEA TATUM, MARRIED 24 YEARS

# CULTURE SHOCK

*Be kind and compassionate to one another,*
*forgiving each other, just as in Christ God forgave you.*
EPHESIANS 4:32

## HE SAYS

Moving to Texas from anywhere else in the world creates its own unique brand of culture shock. They call us "Texas transplant survivors" for a reason. For instance, I *thought* we liked sports in Tennessee, but in Texas amateur and professional athletics are elevated to an almost spiritual level. Games involve shouting matches and shoving—and that's just in the church leagues!

Another adjustment I had to make was to the spiciness of Lone Star food. Where I grew up, if it got much hotter than regular table pepper, we reached for the water. In Texas it's quite common to see someone breaking out in a sweat, not from the temperature of the restaurant but from the copious amounts of Scorned Woman or Straight from Below sauce they're ingesting. Years of eating like this must burn the taste buds off the tongue. How else could one endure such pain? Call me a wimp, but when my nose gets singed from just smelling food, my natural reflux. . .I mean, reflex. . .is to turn and run.

When Dena and I got married and moved to Texas, I had a different kind of culture shock—one of the nuptial variety. We were madly in love, but let's be honest. When you actually start living with someone, you make a boatload of adjustments: which way the toilet paper comes off the holder, where to set the thermostat, which way to squeeze the toothpaste tube. These are small things, for sure. However, like ants, one or two areas of culture shock aren't that bad, but dozens can leave you itching for relief.

## SHE SAYS

I didn't expect the amount of culture shock I felt after getting married. After all, Carey and I had so much in common: values, family size, church backgrounds, education, future dreams and goals. Who knew that marriage would require a million little adjustments every time we were together?

For example, we'd never driven much in a real car before we were hitched. We spent two years in an RV, mostly driven by other mission team members. I didn't realize that Carey suffered from SDD: severe directional dyslexia. After six months of marriage, he still couldn't find his way from our apartment to the church we joined—and they were on the exact same street! I blew up at him (on the way to worship God, of course) after the umpteenth time he turned the wrong way. I truly thought he was doing it on purpose. Turns out, he simply needs either a map or a navigator—or both. Thank God for the advent of cell phones and GPS!

As Carey said, little things can become big things if you don't talk about them. Early on we learned to ask questions, listen to the other person's viewpoint, and—if necessary—agree to disagree. We also implemented a phrase that has often saved us from plummeting into all-out spousal warfare: "Your way is not worse or better than mine; it's just different."

You're free to use the phrase, too. Believe me, it will come in handy.

*Father, thank You for the uniqueness of my spouse. Forgive me when I get impatient with the way he/she does things. Give me patience and grace in those times. Help me step back, take a deep breath, and realize that we are combining cultures and melding two different lifestyles.*

## TAKING OFF THE GLOVES

- What little differences between the two of you have been the hardest to accept?
- Why do you do things the way you do? Talk about the ways you grew up.
- The next time you're frustrated by your spouse's habits, practice saying, "Your way is not worse or better than mine; it's just different." See if it helps diffuse the situation.

### TIPS FROM THE PROS

*Pray for your partner out loud. Let your partner hear your petitions, praise, and thanksgiving for them. Send or leave them little encouraging notes throughout the day. Let them know, no matter what, you are on their side and you have their back.*
—Connie Leonard, married 45 years

# WHEN OPPOSITES ATTACK

*Therefore shall a man leave his father and his mother,*
*and shall cleave unto his wife: and they shall be one flesh.*
GENESIS 2:24 KJV

## SHE SAYS

When I was "in like" with Carey and he saw me as just a buddy, I moaned to a mutual friend, "It would be easier if I got tired of him! But I never do."

(Insert laughter here.)

Ah, young love. It's so innocent, so fervent, so unrealistic. I thought doing mission work with my sweetheart would be similar to sharing a home with him.

While I still love my husband more than words can express, it took only a few months of 24/7 togetherness for me to nearly run out the door screaming. After all, I dislike crowds; he thrives in them. I'm a free spirit; he's a planner. I'm low energy and he's high energy. You get the idea.

Opposites attract, right? Well, after a few years of marriage, they can also attack.

As comedienne Rita Rudner says, "I love being married. It's so great to find that one special person you want to annoy for the rest of your life."

Many marriages end up like the majority of television couples, in which the wife and husband constantly "dig" at each other about their various faults. I don't want to have that kind of relationship—and thankfully, neither does Carey.

So, the question is, how can we keep from plummeting down into negativity, especially after several years together? In our experience, we can consistently be for—and not against—each other only with supernatural help. God can give us the strength, patience, and unconditional love not only to put up with our spouses but to celebrate them.

## HE SAYS

The bridge spanning engagement to married life crosses a wide canyon. Suddenly you go from being wide-eyed, crazy in love with someone you thought you knew pretty well to actually living with that person—*all the time.*

Becoming one flesh didn't just magnify the blissful parts of being together; it also intensified our differences.

One of the reasons God allows us to experience hardships is to remind us of our reliance on Him. In other words, if marriage is difficult, it's that way for a reason. God wants to use your union, even with all its speed bumps, to make you both more like Him.

God is very economical in relationships; in other words, He uses every part of your (and your spouse's) makeup. Once Dena and I discovered how to get in step with the new rhythm of a life built together, we found we could even *benefit* from each other's differences.

For instance, if there is something in our life that calls for precision and detail, I usually step up—and Dena likes that. When we face a situation that takes emotional finesse and discernment, Dena is better suited to lead the way.

In this way, "The two shall become one" takes on new meaning. I'm able to flourish better with Dena than without her. As a matter of fact, that's one of the main ways you know you've found "the one." When you realize in a dating relationship that you can more effectively answer God's calling on your life with this person—warts and all—than without them, you've found a special bond.

*Father, thank You for the bond we share. Help us see the positive in the ways we complement one another instead of immediately feeling frustrated when our personalities clash. Forgive us when we strike out or seek our own comfort and convenience first, instead of humbly seeking to understand (and be understood).*

## TAKING OFF THE GLOVES

- Talk about some of your personal quirks and personality traits. Laugh together about the ways God created you to be so different. (Helpful hint: if you start to argue or get too frustrated, back off and return to the topic later.)
- Think about times when your spouse handled something much better than you did. Is there a way you could incorporate his or her wisdom into that area on a regular basis?
- Men and women have different wiring—and that can be frustrating to the opposite sex. Talk about stereotypes for each sex (all women love to shop; real men don't eat quiche), and discuss how each of you matches (or doesn't match) that generality.

## TIPS FROM THE PROS

*Couples can spend a lifetime of fruitless, unhappy years trying to change each other to mirror their own personalities instead of celebrating and being grateful for their differences. Remember, men and women are different—and love does cover a multitude of flaws!*

—REBECCA BARLOW JORDAN, MARRIED 49 YEARS

# FAMILY TRADITIONS

*"So whatever you wish that others would do to you,
do also to them, for this is the Law and the Prophets."*
Matthew 7:12 ESV

## HE SAYS

The melding of family traditions often blindsides many newlyweds. Rarely do we realize we are marrying into a flood of "that's not how I grew up doing it."

He grew up not making a big deal about birthdays. She grew up with Martha Stewart–worthy parties every year. He remembers Christmas Eve at home by the fireplace. She waxes nostalgic about cruising the town while looking at Christmas lights. . .and so on and so forth.

My first reality check with Dena's traditions of yore came when I attended a family reunion on her side. Growing up, my own family reunions were in someone's front yard. We set up tables loaded with enough food to kill a team of oxen. Next, we'd exchange niceties with folks that we love but rarely see, not drawing attention to the fact that we'd forgotten our third cousin's name and greeting them with an enthusiastic "Hey, man!" Then, after eating an amount that can only be described as "antisocial," we sat in lawn chairs, unbuttoned the top buttons of our pants to relieve pressure, and cycled in and out of nodding off and chatting about (1) southeastern US weather patterns or (2) any surgical procedures we'd endured since the last reunion.

Big family gatherings on Dena's side were similar to mine only because there were people there and they all breathed air. Besides that, the term *polar opposite* comes to mind. Dena's side of the family stayed at a retreat center in cabins. . .for five days. . .*together.*

Food was a necessary afterthought, not elevated to deity status like I was used to. And there were no casual games of horseshoes going on. No, Dena comes from a long line of competitive people. I entered the conference room and found a whiteboard full of sports brackets to rival an NCAA tournament. And yes, there were trophies for the winners. Needless to say, no one "got me" when I showed my appendectomy scar.

## SHE SAYS

Another tradition that tripped us up at first was the different ways our families of origin celebrated special occasions. My mother outdid herself on every birthday, making elaborate gifts and treats from scratch. From sunup until sundown, the special person was made to feel like royalty. In Carey's family, however, a card and small gift sufficed.

On my first birthday after getting married, I expected to be treated like the queen I was. Carey, bless his heart, had no clue that my expectations were so high.

Cue the dramatic music.

We "discussed" traditions quite a bit after that—very intensely. In order to save other couples from the same marital train wreck we suffered, we offer the following advice:

First, somewhere between planning the wedding and picking out curtains, every engaged couple should take an afternoon and talk about holidays and special occasions. Walk through one calendar year together and clarify each other's expectations.

Second, be willing to compromise and change for the sake of unity. (This advice applies to every area of marriage, not just holidays.) Jesus calls us to sacrifice our own desires and treat our spouse as we would want to be treated. How can you honor your mate's wishes without breaking the bank—or your neck? If you are the one with higher expectations, give grace to your partner.

Third, come up with traditions of your own. (Carey laughs at me because if we do something more than once, I call it a tradition. But I love creating new ones!) Brainstorm new ways to celebrate. Encompass your unique personalities, favorite foods, and activities.

And finally, have fun!

*Creator, You have given us such different backgrounds. Thank You for the diversity of experiences and insights You've instilled in us. Make us more like You, Lord—selfless and sacrificial—when we come up against high expectations about family traditions.*

## TAKING OFF THE GLOVES

- Are there specific holidays or special occasions that have caused hurt feelings or conflict in the past? Talk about a time when one of you felt ignored or let down.

- Have you created traditions of your own? If so, talk about them. If not, get creative. How could you personalize your next celebration?
- The next time you're with extended family members, ask them where some of your childhood traditions came from.

## TIPS FROM THE PROS

*Greg and I both see glimpses of the child we once were in each other,
and we treat that child with tenderness and great affection.*
—BECKY JOHNSON, MARRIED 12 YEARS

# COMBINING FAMILY CULTURES

*Let the peace of Christ keep you in tune with each other, in step with each other.*
*None of this going off and doing your own thing.*
COLOSSIANS 3:15 MSG

## SHE SAYS

A strong, healthy marriage is built on communication, compromise, and cooperation, because when a man and woman say "I do," they combine cultures. I'm not just talking about interracial marriage, or marriage in which the husband and wife come from vastly different backgrounds.

Carey and I were raised much the same—in conservative Christian, smallish families with one brother each. Our families had middle-class incomes, fathers who built their own businesses, and moms who stayed at home. Every marriage, however, includes the union of two different cultures, because each family of origin has its own habits, pace, and lifestyle.

A few weeks or months into their union—especially if the husband or wife hasn't lived with other people before—culture shock begins to set in. Each spouse may wonder, *What have I gotten myself into?* They can become homesick for a unique way of life they'd never even noticed before.

My sweetie's family members all have tons of energy and love to keep busy. My clan is much quieter and more laid-back. When we were first married, Carey's preferred pace of living wore me out. I couldn't keep up, and I didn't really want to.

Both of us had to learn to adjust when we found ourselves out of our element.

## HE SAYS

I come from a long line of hyper people. To be sure, there are generations of Dyers with undiagnosed ADD. I don't believe in all of that "spirit animal" mumbo jumbo, but if I did, mine would be the rabid squirrel. It's a wonder Dena ever made the leap with me, as she is. . .I forget what you people call it. . .*sane.*

How does this manifest itself in our marriage? Well, when Dena and I take the kids for a visit to my hometown in Tennessee, we know to get ready to wear ourselves out having fun. You see, with all of that hyperness, I grew up in a family of doers. Visit aunts and uncles, go to the movies, run to the bookstore, drive by every school I attended, hit a bucket of balls at the driving range, get down the old photo albums, now. . .lunch! Those visits are fun, for sure; but it's the kind of fun where you fall at the finish line—full of food and great memories.

Words can hardly express how different visits to Dena's hometown are. When I first visited the idyllic ranch where Dena grew up, I spun in like the Tasmanian devil—only to find things almost ground to a halt. Sleeping in is the norm. A late breakfast might be followed by just sitting around for a couple of hours, reading and talking. Maybe by late afternoon a couple of folks will take a stroll out to see the horses, while the others catch a little nap. After a couple of days, I innocently asked Dena, "So, honey, is this what you guys do? Just kinda sit around?"

Over time, Dena and I have learned to get into the current of our respective families' flow—whether it's a raging river or a gentle stream. We've also met in the middle with our own family dynamics. I've slowed my roll, and Dena has learned to "rev up" when she needs to.

It's a metaphor for our whole marriage relationship, really. We love each other, and we're in it for the long haul. So we engage in give-and-take.

It's called becoming one.

*Father, give us oneness of purpose and spirit. You set the example for us in the Trinity, three distinct beings—Father, Son, Spirit—who live and move in complete unity and agreement. May the peace of Christ keep us in tune with one another, and may we make beautiful music together.*

## TAKING OFF THE GLOVES

- What ways have your different backgrounds caused conflict? Try to laugh about them instead of allowing them to become thorns in your sides.
- How have you compromised in your daily routines or activities?
- Try to create your own traditions as soon after marriage as you can. (Don't wait to until you have children create special milestones. Plan creative outings, try new hobbies, or travel together as a couple.)

## TIPS FROM THE PROS

*Pick your fights. Some things are worth fighting about and some are not. Be choosy. And always say "I love you" at the end of the day.*
—JESSLYN BRAZELL, MARRIED 54 YEARS

# WE ARE ALL HOARDERS

*"In the original creation, God made male and female to be together. Because of this, a man leaves father and mother, and in marriage he becomes one flesh with a woman—no longer two individuals, but forming a new unity."*
MARK 10:5–9 MSG

## HE SAYS

We like stacks. Neat stacks, mind you, but stacks just the same. I have stacks of bills in my office, piles of music yet to be played, heaps of home-made holiday offerings from my little artists, and mounds of books (of which I've read the first three chapters). Dena is into stacks as well—magazines on her nightstand, notes and papers to be signed or graded, and a junk drawer full of pens that no longer write.

Perhaps our most perpetual pile, however, is the worn-once-but-not-quite-dirty clothes on the end of my bed. In my opinion, our bed's footboard had never really found its purpose until I discovered how well its shape lends itself to neatly stacking multiple shirts and pants.

> Dena: Honey, your clothes are piling up again.
> Me: If I'm gonna wear them again, why hang them up? (Right?)

I would need another book to describe the stacks and piles in my sons' rooms. Suffice it to say, they like stacks, too—and unlike the adults in our family, my younger boy's stacks sometimes involve organic materials, including (but not limited to) half-eaten PBJs on his DVDs.

I can Google "clutter" and find several pages of entries on how to properly store items, how to declutter my closet (and how this is a metaphor for decluttering my emotional life), and how the Container Store has a sale on translucent tote boxes. That's all fine and dandy, for sure. But honestly, I like our stacks. We don't let them get out of control, and they seem to give our home some personality.

Maybe the articles are right, though. In a way, my life is a big mental, spiritual, and emotional stack. Sometimes it's neat and most everything seems in order, but more often than not, there are things that are awry—even some that I've allowed to collect dust. I think God is okay with our stacks. He can handle them and will guide us through the parts that need to be tended. After all, if *everything* was in place, life wouldn't be very interesting, would it?

## SHE SAYS

When Carey and I got engaged, he turned to me one day and said, "Know what I just figured out? When we get married, we get each other's stuff!"

I nodded. "Yes," I replied, "that's true." At the time, we were living on a $250 per month stipend each and had been—only months before—college students, so I hated to break it to him: all I owned in the world was a stack of contemporary Christian CDs, some hand-me-down furniture, and a used car.

His stack of loot wasn't much better, but after spending twenty-four months living out of a suitcase, we were happy to have a small apartment with just enough space for our worn couch, "heirloom" table and chairs, and a few pieces of childhood bedroom furniture. (We pooled our savings and bought a bed together. That made us feel so grown-up and responsible!)

Twenty years into this deal, I sigh in resignation. We get each other's stuff. Not only do I share in Carey's paycheck (yay!) and health benefits (double yay!) but I also share in his moods, hang-ups, and insecurities. I get to (clearing throat) *enjoy* his habits, such as biting his fingernails and spitting them out. Gross.

And then there's the kids and their stuff. Our two boys are both collectors. I looked that word up in my handy-dandy mom dictionary, and it said: "Collector. Noun. A person who never ever throws anything away, especially if it has little to no monetary or sentimental value. This person's room stays in a state of dustiness and disrepair. Also see: hoarder."

Truth be told, we all hoard things—prejudices and blind spots, personal quirks and faulty beliefs, even lies Satan has thrown at us through other people and devastating circumstances.

That's one reason we should have gone to more than one premarital counseling session. At the time, we were so in love we couldn't imagine anything getting in the way of our complete devotion to God and each other. A few years in, we could have used a few tools in our belt, both financially and relationally.

Never be ashamed to ask for help. It might make all the difference!

*Jesus, thank You for the mystery of oneness in marriage. We confess*
*that there are times when our baggage gets in the way of unity.*
*Help us let go when we hold onto things we should release.*

## TAKING OFF THE GLOVES

- What aspects of each other's lives did you enjoy sharing when you married your spouse?
- What things disappointed or surprised you?
- How have you grown together since the day you said "I do"?
- How could you grow even closer?

### TIPS FROM THE PROS

*Don't let the romance die. Respect each other.*
*And have separate bathrooms.*
—JOHN PHOENIX McCAULEY, MARRIED 53 YEARS

# THE "UGH" OF MOVING

*He doesn't play hide-and-seek with us. He's not remote; he's near.*
*We live and move in him, can't get away from him!*
ACTS 17:28 MSG

## HE SAYS

Moving. . .ugh. If you've been married for five or more years, chances are you've experienced the bliss of having to move all of your belongings to another place. It's really not that bad, in the same way that it's really not that bad to remove your lung through your left nostril.

I always admired Ruth for telling Naomi, "Whither thou goest, I will go." Of course, Ruth didn't have an entertainment center the size of a Buick, but still.

We have moved seven times, which ironically is the number of perfection. Every time we've moved, we've had the same conversation about getting rid of all of the stuff that we never use; but alas, there it remains when it comes time for the next move—sometimes still in the box from the previous relocation. "I really *am* going to start using this pull-up bar, seriously."

Heads up: although you'll be tempted to have a garage sale before moving, don't give in. I can't explain it, but no matter how much merchandise you have, by the time you take a day off from work and make the pizza run for lunch, you'll always clear exactly twenty-four dollars. A trip to the Goodwill store is much easier; plus you won't get awakened by the professional "yard sale people" (googly-eyed creatures who arrive at your house one full hour before the advertised time, carrying a sock full of quarters).

Loading and hauling tons of belongings aren't the only chores that take their toll. Getting your cable, utilities, and Wi-Fi changed over is just slightly less time consuming than moving a sand pile with a pair of tweezers. And unless you use the Internet, changing the address on your driver's license means taking a lovely trip to your local DMV office, where you wait in a line reminiscent of Disneyland's "It's a Small World" ride (but instead of the perpetual song, there is a perpetual smell).

Interestingly enough, the cost of an address change for two people? Around twenty-four dollars.

## SHE SAYS

I've decided that moving is a lot like childbirth:

- You both dread it and look forward to it.
- You think you can do it all on your own until you realize how exhausting and stressful it is.
- And, finally:
  You forget the pain of the experience and want to repeat it again a few years later.

Every move we've undertaken has been necessary, but during the process, I always have at least one meltdown, in which I sob uncontrollably and beg Carey to tell me *again* the reasons we're doing this stupid, stupid thing. He always reminds me that we will get settled—eventually—and we won't be surrounded by boxes forever.

After one move, in which we downsized to an apartment for about a year, Jackson (who was six years old at the time) kept asking when we could get a house. I finally realized he didn't remember our previous move, which had occurred three years prior. The poor thing thought that apartment dwelling meant living with stacks of musty boxes. . .for as long as you lived there. As soon as I unpacked his things and removed the boxes from his room, he relaxed.

What a great object lesson for marriage! When Carey and I were first wed, we didn't realize the baggage we brought to the union. Our hurts, mistakes, and regrets needed to be unpacked before God could heal us. (And His healing is a work in progress—much like creating the ideal home.)

When we became less encumbered by our pasts, Carey and I were able to move forward into the present—and the future—with more peace and joy. As we live freely and lightly, our hang-ups don't trip us up as often. . .and we are able to connect with each other on a deeper, more meaningful level.

*Lord, it's in You that we live, move, and have our being. Thank You for being constant and unchanging in our ever-changing world. We praise You for the ways You help us unpack our wounds. Heal us from the pain of the past so we can move forward into greater intimacy with You and our spouses.*

## TAKING OFF THE GLOVES

- How many times have you moved (if ever)? Which part of the experience did you enjoy? Which part did you find most stressful?
- Did the story of Jackson and his boxes resonate with you? What things might you have packed away that God wants to bring out in the open?
- Pray together about any baggage you have. Ask Him to move in and through your union, to heal and restore you and your spouse.

## TIPS FROM THE PROS

*If your spouse is irritating you, find all the good things about him and go tell someone. The more you praise your spouse in the presence of others (whether your spouse is there to hear it or not), the more you are able to let go of anger and irritation.*

—KAREN SAWYER, MARRIED 28 YEARS

# NOTES

# NOTES

# PART 2

# TREATING OUR WOUNDS

# MARRIAGE ON MISSION

*As iron sharpens iron, so one person sharpens another.*
PROVERBS 27:17

## SHE SAYS

In college I read a book by Ken Abraham on finding a godly mate (in my opinion, almost everything meaningful can be learned by reading). I don't remember much about the book, but one thought stood out to me, and it's something I've told my sons and other young people who've asked me about marriage.

Basically, Ken said that you've found the right person to marry when your ministry will be more powerful together than it would be if you ministered separately.

Such a thought excited me, because God called me into ministry at the age of eleven. At the time, I believed I had to be either a missionary in Africa or a church staff member. Since then, however, His unique plans for me have taken shape—and I've been amazed at the varied paths He has led me down.

Carey and I met through full-time ministry. Since getting married, we've tried to stay open and obedient to the call of God, wherever it would take us. Separately and together, He has allowed us to serve on many different mission teams; lead music and worship in churches; write articles and books; teach, speak, and mentor others; and perform in professional theater productions.

What makes ministering together even more special? We are truly a team. God put us together to complement each other rather than compete with each other. We rejoice in each other's success and serve as each other's biggest fans. We feel excited about the future because with the Lord, there really are no limits.

## HE SAYS

Speaking of competition, in my high school cafeteria, I sat at the marching band table, which—in the hierarchy of teenage social strata—was well below varsity jocks and slightly above cart-pushing freshman. I actually loved band, the ever-present "band geek" nickname notwithstanding. As a matter of fact, I feel a sense of nostalgia when I run into a fellow band member and have been known to obsessively watch the annual DCI World Marching Band Championships on PBS.

Don't judge.

In a similar but less nerdy way, I feel a sense of camaraderie when I come across married couples. When the guy in front of me in the checkout line is obviously buying something for his wife, or when I find myself sitting on the same clothing store bench with a guy who is also waiting for his sweetie, the topic of marriage is a good conversation starter, a nice launch pad for getting to know someone.

Committed, lasting marriage is often mocked in our culture—"ball and chain" is a phrase that gets sometimes used when the subject comes up. But Dena and I try to encourage folks who are engaged or already wed that the years after saying "I do" can be fulfilling and fun.

Your union might even be something that God wants to use in the lives of others. Have you two ever considered yourself "on mission" together? I'm not referring to an uber couple, professionally trained in counseling, who exist in a state of relationship nirvana. (I'm pretty sure those people don't exist.) However, God could use the wisdom you've gained, and even the scars you've developed along the way, to help those just starting out.

Similarly, have you considered finding a "mentor couple," two people older and wiser, who seem to be pacesetters for a good marriage? Dena and I cherish spending time with George and Ruthie. We only see them from time to time, but when we do, we always come away refreshed and inspired by their bond.

Like anything else in your lives together, I urge you to be deliberate about building relationships with other couples. God may want to use your marriage to sharpen others' unions—and you are wise to spend time with those men and women who can sharpen yours.

*Lord, show us how to be married "on mission." Open up opportunities for us to mentor younger couples and to be mentored by more experienced couples. As we walk with the wise, may we become wise.*

## TAKING OFF THE GLOVES

- What might having a "marriage on mission" look like for you and your spouse?
- Do you know of a younger couple you could encourage?

- Think about older couples you admire. What is it about their union that inspires you?
- Might they be willing to mentor you, even unofficially?

## TIPS FROM THE PROS

*Looking back, it's amazing to see how we have grown together. He always calls me "Beautiful," and he is my "handsome prince." I love how we have grown in Christ and hope we can be an encouragement to others. Forty-one years of perfection? Of course not! But forty-one years of true love!*
—DIANE BALL, MARRIED 41 YEARS

# SPIRITUAL LEADERSHIP

*Husbands, love your wives and do not be harsh with them.*
COLOSSIANS 3:19

## SHE SAYS

When I was single, I read several preparing-for-marriage books by Christian authors. I was also blessed with godly female mentors. I'm truly thankful for the influence these wise believers had in my life; however, there is one specific piece of advice I wish I had read or heard: *There is more than one way for a husband to be a spiritual leader.*

To the women in my Christian circles, the ideal husband would not only regularly pray with us, but he would also serve as our accountability partner, read the Bible with us, lead daily devotions (with the children, too, when they came along), attend church regularly, tithe, and serve on church committees and in leadership. He might even plan regular family mission trips! Basically, we were looking for our very own spiritual Superman.

Please hear me: I'm not saying that Christian husbands shouldn't lead devotions for their families or pray with their wives. On the contrary—I think those are wonderful actions to take! I'm just saying that many times, we women harbor unrealistic standards for our mates.

Then, because our superhigh standards are impossible for men to achieve, Satan invites us to camp out in Poor Me-Ville—a place of discouragement, disillusionment, and discontentment.

Instead of pressuring your spouse to do certain things—which might leave him feeling guilty and insecure—encourage him when he reaches out spiritually, via conversation or action, with you or others. Pray for him, fervently and specifically, every day. And realize that you will grow in your faith (and the ways you express that faith) at different paces.

## HE SAYS

*Spiritual leader.* Perhaps no two words struck more fear in my heart when I first considered marriage. I had heard that term thrown around (and perhaps misused) so much in relation to men in the home that I was intimidated, to say the least. First of all, if you can't tell by what I've written thus far, I tend to be pretty lighthearted and, well, silly. I've never been one of those deep, introverted, brooding thinkers who plumbs the depths of spiritual richness and smells of pipe tobacco and old leather. Sometimes I feel like a chicken tender in a duck à l'orange world. However, here are three one-bite appetizers for leading out in the home:

1. *Hey, hubby, it ain't your show.* I like this quote from author, speaker, and theologian John Piper: "I define spiritual leadership as knowing where God wants people to be and taking the initiative to use God's methods to get them there in reliance on God's power."[1]

Did you notice how many times the emphasis is on God and not on you? The key is reliance on His power. Whenever I think that effectiveness in leading my family rests in my own strength or personality, the Lord reminds me that He alone can equip me for what He has called me to do.

2. *Drill sergeants are for the military.* Having a "my way or the highway" attitude is a great way to bring division into your home. The apostle Paul likened a man's role to Christ as head of the church (Ephesians 5:23). My aim should be gentleness, compassion, and a respect for the members of my family. If someone feels belittled, I need to rethink my game plan. It's hard to give TLC when you're being a CEO.

3. *Take a few deep breaths.* Step off the perfection hamster wheel and relax a bit. Setting the spiritual pace for our family is a journey. Rest in God's grace, apologize when you say or do something to cause offense, and keep moving forward. Your wife and kids are going to remember your heart more than your methods. Just having a *desire* to lean on Jesus and lead your family to Him puts you on the right path.

To put it rather simply: invest in them as He invests in you.

For husbands: *God, I want to lead my family to grow in Your grace and in the knowledge of You. Help me seek so hard after You that my family can't help but be drawn to You, too. Forgive me when I've failed in this area. Thank You for the example Jesus set in His love for the church.*

For wives: *Father, give me Your eyes to see how my husband tries to be a leader in our family. Forgive me when I've been too hard on him. Remind me to pray for him and encourage the efforts he's making.*

---

1. John Piper, *The Marks of a Spiritual Leader* (Minneapolis: Desiring God, 2014), 3

## TAKING OFF THE GLOVES

- Take turns affirming each other about specific ways you've seen spiritual growth in the other person.
- Make a spiritual "wish list" together. What things would you like to do as a family to encourage each member to grow spiritually? Some examples: serving together locally or globally, having a family worship service once a month, sitting together in church.
- Start a prayer journal—or prayer box (filled with blank index cards)—as a couple. Leave it on your kitchen counter or on a bedside table, and jot down prayer needs as they come to mind. This way, whether or not you pray together, you can lift up each other's needs (and those of others you know and love) regularly.

## TIPS FROM THE PROS

*Serve them. Love them through action, even when you don't want to.*
*Pray together. Ask routinely what they're struggling with*
*in their walk with God and what they're studying.*
—MATT BUFKIN, MARRIED 11 YEARS

# "QUIET TIMES" FOR COUPLES

*But they delight in the law of the LORD,*
*meditating on it day and night.*
PSALM 1:2 NLT

## SHE SAYS

I learned to spend regular time with God during a summer church camp experience. The speaker mentioned the phrase "quiet time," and when I grasped what it meant, I decided I needed to implement it in my own life. As an introverted teen and a college student, I enjoyed praying, journaling, and reading scripture and devotional books, and Jesus truly became a friend and not just a complicated, unreachable being.

But. . .

Most people who talk about this spiritual practice insist the only correct time with God is first thing after waking. Evidently scholars have discovered evidence that David, Jesus, and Paul jumped out of bed singing, "Rise and shine and give God the glory, glory!"

In contrast, my favorite morning hymn is "In the morning when I rise, give me coffee." Therefore, I've had the most meaningful experiences with God later in the day. The first thing I do when I hear the alarm is hit the snooze button. Then when I do rise, I search out my morning cup of java. Jesus, Carey, my kids, the dog—they are no less important to me just because they don't filter into my consciousness before caffeine sets in. It's just body chemistry, not spirituality.

I've learned to work with the way my Creator made me instead of fighting it. This approach leads to much less guilt and much more joy. I've also learned to pray for Carey instead of trying to force him to lead us both in prayer or reading scripture. When he turns to me and says, "Let's pray," I rejoice and thank God for that moment. When he doesn't, I remember all the other quiet, gentle ways he leads us. Those virtues—consistency, loyalty, devotion, gratitude, humor—are not often celebrated by a Christian culture that revels in loud, larger-than-life leaders.

## HE SAYS

Dena and I have not always been consistent about having a devotional time together. Part of the struggle stems from my own "issues" with the guilt-laden words *quiet time.*

Like Dena, I grew up in an ultraconservative bubble, and the phrase smacked of getting up before the roosters and reading a certain number of verses for a set number of minutes—like a spiritual SAT exam. I bought into the legalistic formula hook, line, and sinker. *If a spastic monkey like me can sit on his hands for thirty minutes and be still, surely that proves my devotion to God,* I mused.

However, as I think about the ways my boys enjoy time with me—wrestling on the floor, laughing to the point of pain, going on daring pirate adventures that span the seven seas of our backyard—I wonder if I spend too much time stressing about something that should be a very natural occurrence. What if a "quiet time" is as easy as speaking Jesus' name, expressing my love for Him, and seeing what timeless truth He wants to show me in His Word on that day?

Nowadays, whether it's alone or with Dena, I like my personal time with God to be less about rules and more about freely expressing myself to God at that particular moment, whatever form it takes. Will it often involve reading scripture? Yes, of course. But it might also include hitting a bike trail and having my own little adventure in God's backyard. Or maybe I'll light a candle that smells like banana cream pie and write out a big thank-you note to Him.

Many times my morning walk with Dena starts out as a way to keep the pounds off and ends up being a time when we can share our burdens and dreams—a prayer list to go by as we think of each other throughout the day.

Of course, it's not about me; it's about pleasing Him. But what could please the Father more than seeing His children bask in His presence with abandon?

I don't think God likes to be put in a box (I know I don't). And although being quiet and still before Him definitely has its place, it's not the only way to express our hearts to God. So think outside the box—I believe that's where He hangs out. And as you seek the Lord, exercise the uniqueness that He created in you—even if that means the two of you spending some unquiet time with Him.

*Abba Father, we adore You and want to spend time with You, both separately and together. Forgive us for making it about checklists and formulas. Remind us of the joy we first felt when You called us to Your side. Give us creative ideas for spending time with You, and help us to rest in Your love.*

## TAKING OFF THE GLOVES

- Have you heard the phrase "quiet time"? What does it mean to each of you?
- Do you pray and read scripture regularly together or separately? Why or why not?
- Talk about ways you could incorporate prayer and/or scripture into your day. Be creative!

## TIPS FROM THE PROS

*The thing I cherish most about my wife is that God brought us together. Amy is the best for me because of God's design for us—that us-ness is what makes us unique.*
—JIMMIE STORRIE, MARRIED 27 YEARS

# NEVER DOWN FOR THE COUNT

*An intelligent heart acquires knowledge,*
*and the ear of the wise seeks knowledge.*
PROVERBS 18:15 ESV

## HE SAYS

Dena is a fine cook. . .now. When we were newlyweds, though, not so much. I don't know exactly what words would adequately describe Dena's cooking prowess (or lack thereof) during those first couple of years. Perhaps I could paint the picture for you with a couple of quotes taken straight from our small apartment kitchen:

"No, honey, I think you're supposed to brown the meat and *then* add it to the spaghetti sauce."

"Dear, I'm pretty sure that you should have removed that paper liner from the store-bought pie crust *before* you poured the quiche mixture in."

"Sweetie, is this Cajun fish? 'Cause mine's blackened."

(Smoke alarm going off) Dena: "Dinner's ready!"

I honestly think her early failures in the kitchen were rooted in one of her strengths. Dena is an ambitious, let's-get-this-done-quickly-and-efficiently person. So, if something was supposed to be baked at 350 degrees for twenty minutes, it made perfect sense to Dena that she could get it done in ten minutes. . .if she could bake it at 700 degrees. ("Honey, I think our kitchen walls are melting again.")

In all seriousness, my cute little chef has come a long way. Start with a few years of watching the Food Network during every waking moment, fold in some culinary ideas from Pinterest, add a few cups of trial-and-error, stir it all together—and you've got a recipe for a pretty good cook. Sometimes I'll even jump in and help. We've made cooking a way to spend time together and talk about our day.

I look back on the genesis of our married relationship with such fondness. I usually walked home for lunch from my job at the seminary bookstore (looking like Dwight from *The Office*, with my tie and short-sleeved, colored dress shirt). We'd sit at the kitchen table, which was actually in our living room, gaze into each other's eyes, and share a romantic lunch of boxed macaroni and cheese. On special occasions, we'd add sliced hot dogs to the mix.

But you know what? We were perfectly content, blissful even. Whether or not we knew enough to verbalize it, we realized we had what mattered most. We never thought twice about my low-paying job, our Goodwill furniture, or Dena's "extra-crispy" bacon. We were basking in the glow of our young love.

## SHE SAYS

First off, my husband just got brownie points for calling me "cute," "little," and "chef." Nice!

Those early years were sweet—even though my cooking wasn't.

But learning to cook was necessary after Carey took on a full-time ministry position a few years ago. (He had been the family meal planner and maker; I was more than happy to be on cleanup duty.) Still, I looked forward to developing a new skill. Watching my favorite cooking shows had demystified a process that once seemed overwhelming. "I can do this," I told myself.

I just had to follow instructions—not something I'm particularly fond of.

However, as I followed recipes and found initial success, my confidence grew. Having our sons and Carey compliment me on dishes I made with my own hands was new—and gratifying. Once I found a rhythm, I even enjoyed the planning, shopping, and cooking process. It was a completely different way to be creative. When I got stuck on a book project, I chopped, simmered, and baked to clear my mind. And after I was done, unlike some of my writing, the meal didn't get rejected. Instead, it was consumed with enjoyment and appreciation (most of the time).

There was also something immensely satisfying about proving to myself that I could conquer a long-standing fear. In order to learn to cook, I needed to silence the inner voice that said, "You're too old to learn a new trick," and "You'll never be good at this." Instead, I believed that God had given me reasonable intelligence and would help me serve my family through providing them with tasty, healthy meals.

The other day, my oldest son told someone, "Mom's learned to cook. She's actually a normal. . .well, she'll never be *normal*, but she cooks well now."

Dear reader, I'll take it.

*Lord, give us patience with those things we're not so good at. Help us encourage rather than belittle each other. May we always seek to grow and change in order to be more like You. Lord, when there's something that would serve and bless our spouse, give us the courage and God-confidence to try it.*

## TAKING OFF THE GLOVES

- Have you learned something new lately, or do you want to learn a new skill? Talk about some steps you could take to develop a new interest or hobby.
- In what areas do you feel defeated by repeated failure? Could you find a different way around the problem? Brainstorm together.
- Put aside an evening to watch the movie *Julie and Julia* together. It's a romantic film about food—and two very different marriages.

### TIPS FROM THE PROS

*1. Commit—never give up.*

*2. Love is a decision. Make a decision to love each other.*

*3. Your spouse is your better half. Treat him/her that way.*

*4. Make an effort to find out what his/her day was like.*

*Even if you have only three minutes to talk, use them.*

—LAURA AND STEVEN HILTON, MARRIED 27 YEARS

# LIVING ON LOVE
## (AND NOT MUCH ELSE)

*"Bring the whole tithe into the storehouse, that there may be food in
my house. Test me in this," says the LORD Almighty, "and see if I
will not throw open the floodgates of heaven and pour out so much
blessing that there will not be room enough to store it."*
MALACHI 3:10

## SHE SAYS

When we were missionaries together—but before we began dating—I
noticed that immediately after getting paid, Carey always wrote a tithe check
and sent it to his home church. That was superattractive to me.

Many single men and women have lists of specific things they're looking
for in an ideal mate, and I was no exception. After dating a few less-than-
stellar boys in college, I had "giver" high on my list of desired qualities.

I had grown up in church, and I knew that God promised to bless those
who gave the firstfruits of their money, time, and resources to Him. I'd seen
it in my own life and my family's life.

I'm glad that tithing was never a question for Carey and me. As my
pastor and friend, Mark Forrest, says: "God can do much more with your 90
percent than you can do with 100."

Amen to that!

## HE SAYS

Music and ministry: "Yes, Alex, I'll take *low-paying career choices* for five
hundred dollars."

The job paths Dena and I have chosen aren't always financially
rewarding. But when one answers God's call, monetary concerns shouldn't
be the deciding factor. That being said, God has always been faithful to meet
our needs, and we are truly thankful for what He has given us. I've traveled a
bit to other countries, and I understand that on the global scene, the average
American is rich indeed.

Like most couples, we've had times when we've saved money wisely and
other times when we had to cross our fingers at the ATM. And debt? Some
months Visa didn't send us a bill. They sent a thank-you note!

I remember when we were a newly married, broke (and I mean *broke*), and "living on love" seminary couple. On the rare occasion when we went out to dinner, we scrounged around for loose change to secure enough funds. If we could come up with $8.68, we could both buy a pizza buffet *and* a soda at a local restaurant. I often think fondly of the childlike joy we found, digging between the car seats until we finally pulled out the quarter that helped us reach the magical amount.

I also remember the day we needed a new kitchen appliance and a check for the right amount "just happened" to appear in the mailbox. Those seem like simpler times, for sure, but I've learned that no matter how many zeroes are at the end of our bank statement, it takes a similar amount of faith, joy, and dependence on the Lord to be generous. Tithing, and going beyond the tithe when God calls us to, is not exactly something the world teaches. That's why it's so important for us to be on the same page about money. When we're unified on important issues, it's so much easier to be countercultural.

People smarter than me say that money is the number one source of marital arguments—and even divorce—in our nation. While finances (or the lack thereof) can be a source of stress, we've found that it can also be a topic that drives us closer to the Lord. He keeps reminding us of three words: dependence, provision, and contentment.

*The world screams at us, "Buy more! Consume more! Take more!" But You ask us to give, and give generously, out of the abundance You've blessed us with. Forgive us when we've been stingy with our money, Lord. Everything we have comes from You. Teach us to depend on You for what we need, and help us find contentment in You, and You alone.*

## TAKING OFF THE GLOVES
- Discuss whether talking about money makes you nervous—and why (if you know the reason).
- As far as spending goes, who is the saver? Who is the spender? (You can both be the same, of course, but many couples who marry are opposites.)
- Who takes care of paying bills? Do both of you agree that this is the best way to handle your finances? Discuss whether any adjustments need to be made.

## TIPS FROM THE PROS

*Discuss managing money before you tie the knot. This is an important topic that should be communicated clearly in advance.*

—DANA ARCURI, MARRIED 26 YEARS

# DECORATING DEBACLE

*The wisest of women builds her house,*
*but folly with her own hands tears it down.*
PROVERBS 14:1 ESV

## HE SAYS

It's hard to describe Dena's eccentric flair for decorating. I don't mind that she likes to change our furniture and accoutrements around more often than others. I've come to expect as much from a creative person like her.

My problem comes with the changes that are, shall we say, more sweeping—such as, I come home from work and think I've entered the wrong house.

When most people pick out a new color, wall décor, or piece of furniture, they tend to take awhile to make the final decision: "Let's sleep on it and see if we still like it in the morning." Well, if you'll pardon my Tennessee vernacular, my wife ain't most people. When she has a flash of decorating inspiration, it skips right past the "Is this practical or doable?" part of her brain. Her ideas even blow right past the "What will it cost to fix it if I mess up?" zone; and don't even get me started on the "Will Carey like it?" filter. That one's been broken for a while. After all, I only live there. Why would I be concerned about how my house looks?

No, no, those brain filters are for the shortsighted, evidently. As soon as Dena *thinks* of an idea, in her mind that gives her the green light to do it—*right now!* "I'll figure it out as I go. How hard can it be?" One day I came home to find inspirational quotes written all over my office wall—in Sharpie, every interior designer's most elegant tool. The words had no guiding lines, no centering or spacing, no light-marked pencil to trace; Dena figured that when taking a permanent marker to my workspace, freehand was the way to go. Needless to say, she agreed that I should paint over it—in bright red paint.

## SHE SAYS

I have to take issue with a few things Carey just said. First of all, there was one quote on the wall. Not several. (It was very poorly executed, though.) Also, I do take his opinion into account about decorating decisions—now, at least. Back then I was of the "a woman's home is her castle" mind-set, and I thought I should be in charge of all decisions related to décor.

I knew I went too far one day when Carey came home to find both couches in different places than they'd been earlier that morning. I had a sheepish expression on my face when he asked, "Who moved them?" He gently chided me for not waiting on him to help move them, and I knew he was right.

Growing up, my parents held very traditional roles. My father brought home the bacon and my mom fried it up. Period. She was in charge of all things house related, and he took care of everything else. Being married to a man who cared about how our home looked took some getting used to, for sure.

Even though we are no longer newlyweds, I still have to stop myself from impulse purchases at Tuesday Morning (unless they're tiny) and remind myself to talk to Carey before redecorating. But I'm glad to do it, because he considers me before making decisions, too.

After all, we are a team, and team members consult one another regularly and communicate honestly—even about paint colors.

*Creator, You made us different, yet You call us to be "one." Give us creative ways to come together. May we show the world a rich and colorful, full-of-laughter-and-life, sold-out-to-Jesus marriage.*

## TAKING OFF THE GLOVES

- What is your decorating style? Have those preferences ever caused conflict?
- Did you grow up with an ultra-traditional model of marriage, in which the man works full-time and the woman stays at home? Or did your parents both work? Maybe you had a single parent or were raised by a family member or in a foster home. Talk about how the way you were raised may have affected your expectations about certain roles and jobs in the home.
- Visit a home improvement and/or home furnishings store on a future date night. Make notes (or take pictures) on your phone about ideas you'd like to try in your own house. Dream together, and have fun doing it.

## TIPS FROM THE PROS

*When you wake up, say, "How can I please God and my spouse today?" and remind yourself of that throughout the day. Live to give—and what you get is pure joy.*

—DEBBIE MURPHY, MARRIED TO TOM
FOR 9 YEARS BEFORE HE PASSED AWAY

# FIGHTING FAIR
# (PART 1)

*"In your anger do not sin": Do not let the sun go down
while you are still angry, and do not give the devil a foothold.*
EPHESIANS 4:26–27

## HE SAYS

I had to learn to play fair in marriage—and when I say, "I had to learn," I mean I'm still learning.

Dena and I know each other well. I know what will make her melt into my arms and what will make her boil with anger. And to be honest, there have been times when I've used this knowledge to manipulate Dena to get what I wanted.

Early in our marriage, if I was really angry, I knew how to light her "mad" fuse, let it sizzle, and *pow!*—emotionally send her through the roof. It was evil and conniving. When we let those old fleshly patterns creep into our relationships, our capacity to hurt someone is quite startling.

Then, as I got a little older (and hopefully wiser), I began to think to myself, *Is the type of arguing Dena and I are engaging in producing the desired results?* In other words, is this really helping, or are we just wearing ourselves out on an emotional treadmill?

Intense disagreements in marriage are unavoidable. In fact, in God's infinite wisdom, He's made it so that arguments can actually lead to growth if we invite Him into the midst of them. I'm not the poster child for complete success, but on my best days, I've learned that the following questions get me closer to Dena—and to God's plan for our marriage:

- *Am I really listening to her?* Even if I disagree with her or feel as if she is completely misunderstanding me, if I *really* listen to her words and (because I know her so well) the heart behind those words, I almost always find nuggets of truth.

- *Am I honoring her?* There's a way to disagree/argue so that the other person is not disrespected. If I resort to sarcasm, eye rolling, or flat-out yelling (all of which I'm pretty "good" at), Dena emotionally shuts down—and rightfully so. At that point, she no longer feels cherished. She no longer feels that I'm loving her enough to find real solutions to our problems. Instead, I've belittled her and made her feel "less than." Friends, that's just wrong. Jesus never makes us feel that way.

Here are some more questions that helped me get closer to Dena and God's plan for marriage:

- *Are we actually getting somewhere?* If you just want to let off steam, go for a run. If you're not learning something about each other or coming up with a game plan for how to grow in and through the situation, then, as the school crossing guard tells Michael Keaton in *Mr. Mom,* "you're doing it wrong."
- *Shall we pray?* This one nails me to the wall, but here goes: Men, if we have an argument/discussion and afterward we don't feel like we can kneel down and pray with our wives, then we need to rethink things. Our spouses are a gift from God, and even on the worst of days, we need to make room for the supernatural in our marriages. We need to seek the Lord's counsel with our wives.
- I want to be sensitive to those who may have a partner who doesn't share their faith (and its heavenly priorities). I'd still encourage you to set the pace in your home by letting your spouse "catch you" praying—and by showing her that even when you disagree, you're committed to treat her with love and respect.

Guys, marriage is not easy, but guess what? It was never supposed to be. The rough patches remind us about how much we need to lean into God. As I've told my kids when they're doing their homework, "Hard is not bad. Hard means you're learning something."

Difficulties and disagreements in our relationships can be outlets for us to "show her who's boss." Or, they can become opportunities for us to surrender to God's guidance and build bridges to a deeper relationship with our beloved.

*Father, we want to have a long, healthy marriage. Teach us how to disagree without demanding our own way. Show us how to argue with respect. You gave us the example of forgiving those who hurt us, Jesus. May we be humble enough to take the first step toward reconciliation, even when we long to retaliate.*

## TAKING OFF THE GLOVES

- Talk honestly about what words, gestures, and facial expressions set each of you off (for Dena, it's sarcasm). Resolve together to avoid shooting those arrows when arguing.
- Laugh together about some of the silly things—restaurants, driving, toilet paper—you've fought over. What's the silliest?
- Pray with each other. Ask God to heal the wounds you've inflicted on each other and to strengthen your bond.

### TIPS FROM THE PROS

*When tension begins to rise, we walk away until we are calmed down. Then we come back together and work out a resolution. We are not in a competition; we are in a loving, long-term marriage, and we desire to honor the Lord God with it.*
—ROBYN BESSEMAN, MARRIED 42 YEARS

# FIGHTING FAIR
## (PART 2)

*What is causing the quarrels and fights among you?*
*Don't they come from the evil desires at war within you?*
JAMES 4:1 NLT

## SHE SAYS

I loved Carey desperately when we first got married, and it shocked me that we would have conflict.

Naive much?

We'd been best friends for a year before we dated and knew each other very well. However, living with someone 24/7, brought out sides of him I'd never seen.

It also brought out sides of *me* I'd never seen. I became self-protective, insecure, and jealous.

Marriage quickly became a crucible (as motherhood would, years later). I realized I had one of two choices: I could either allow God to forgive and free me from my quickly accumulating sins or continue to be selfish and petty.

Some days I chose the latter. On others I chose the former.

I wanted Jesus to have all of me, and I wanted to have a lengthy, healthy marriage. I knew there were no guarantees, except that I—with God's help—could change my own behavior.

Here are a few things I learned about fighting fair:

- *Don't disengage.* My past had taught me to stuff emotions and run from conflict. These were not healthy patterns, and Carey began to force me to stick around when we argued instead of leaving the room or running from issues we needed to work through. Wow, that was painful—but a necessary part of growing up. (By the way, this one took years and lots of hard work. I still tend to "shut down" at times when things get intense. But I'm getting better.)

- *Don't overreact.* In the beginning of our marriage, I often let the way Carey said things send me into a tizzy. Instead of dealing with conflict in emotional, not rational, ways, I had to learn to take a deep breath and listen to Carey's words, not just his tone or presentation. Again, I'm still a work in process.

- *Do find a happy medium.* In the first few years of matrimony, Carey wanted to hash things out for as long as it took to come to an agreement—even if our argument lasted for hours. I wanted to talk about our conflict and then think about it separately, only coming back together when we had cooled down and found some sort of clarity. After a couple of years of butting heads over our differences, we found a compromise that worked for us. We agreed never to go to bed when we were angry, but we also "tabled" certain discussions if I got too fatigued or distraught to continue.

Learning to work through conflicts in marriage is so difficult, entire books have been written on the subject. We've only made a small dent in this important topic, but we hope our foibles have given you fodder for discussion.

One final thought: don't skip over the "making up" part after you've had a fight. It's the best part!

*Father, we don't want to run away from each other or from You, but our desires fight and war within us, and we are tempted to hurt each other. We often choose self-protection over selflessness. Move us from greed to gratitude. Lead us from spite to spiritual union. We need Your help every hour of every day. Continue Your transforming work in us, and sanctify our marriage.*

## TAKING OFF THE GLOVES

- What makes you angry? Jealous? Self-protective? Talk about the ways your spouse could reassure you. Think about ways you can begin to let God heal the wounds that cause those emotions. (For instance, if we've felt abandoned by a parent, certain actions our spouses take—for example, not calling when they'll be late—are often magnified in our minds and lead to angst and anger.)
- When have you surrendered your own desires for the sake of your spouse? How did you feel? How did your spouse react?
- Talk about what it would mean to take the "road less traveled" in marriage.

## TIPS FROM THE PROS

*Never go to bed mad or upset. Be slow to anger and hold your tongue, because at that time, you're more apt to say something you may wish you hadn't. Don't hold on to things from the past or keep score of wrongs.*

—Kayla Freeman, married 10 years

# MEN AND THEIR MOVIES

*And over all these virtues put on love,*
*which binds them all together in perfect unity.*
COLOSSIANS 3:14

## HE SAYS

Occasionally you'll find the two of us sitting in bed, each ear-plugged and staring at our respective laptop screens. However, we're not doing anything productive, like checking Facebook or seeing how many mines we can sweep (he said, sarcastically). Instead, we're pursuing our other "waste large chunks of time" passion: watching movies. We're both film and TV buffs, but we don't always like the same programs; hence, the separate screens.

Recently, I was watching *Rocky III* (the one with the cool music montage training sequence—oh wait, that's all of them). Dena was watching *Downton Abbey* (the one where a wealthy Brit does something mind-numbingly boring and all of the servants talk about it later in the pantry. Is my bias showing?). When we discovered each other's program of choice, we almost simultaneously rolled our eyes.

Before you label me as too shallow (I'm actually just the right amount of shallow), I've been known to take my wife out to watch the occasional "rom-com" or "chick flick." But ladies, you must understand that there lies within a man a ruffian need that can be met only by movies containing plenty of things blowing up, guys overcoming incredible odds, and Whitman-esque barbaric yawping.

So wives everywhere, I implore you. If you have a man caring enough to sit through *Pride and Prejudice* with you when he could be out doing something more enjoyable like, oh, I don't know, poking himself in the eye with a pencil, then by all means, go with him once in a while to see a movie about which the deepest thing you can say afterward is "Cool truck!"

Whether it stars Rachel McAdams or Dwayne Johnson, a movie is a great excuse to spend time with the one you love while eating expensive candy and cheap hot dogs.

## SHE SAYS

Marriage is about give-and-take; not he gives and I take, or vice versa. I don't exactly know why my three guys are so enamored by explosions and car chases, but they are. (John Eldredge wrote about that phenomenon in *Wild at Heart*, but I'm too tired from raising boys to reread it.)

I do share their love of nerdy stuff, especially Harry Potter, Lord of the Rings, *Sherlock*, and *Doctor Who*. When they ask me to watch one of those shows, I readily say yes. And I'm not a big fan of violence for violence's sake, but when I start to get too bent out of shape about the opposite sex's barbaric ways, I remember the Bible—especially the Old Testament—is full of the stuff.

One of my mottos in marriage and parenting is "Choose your battles." We don't allow just any movie into our home, so when Carey or the boys want to watch the latest superhero or dinosaur flick, I don't mind. It allows them to bond and gives me time alone (Hallelujah!). And once in a while, I'll join one or more of them for an outing or sit by Carey on the couch while he watches a "guy" movie.

After all, the popcorn is usually pretty good, and sometimes there's even a plot.

*Lord, thank You for my mate. Help me find things
we can enjoy together and carve out time to do them.*

## TAKING OFF THE GLOVES
- Talk about the freetime activities you each enjoy. Where do you find hobbies/passions that overlap in some way?
- If you don't have any overlap, consider taking up a new interest together such as bowling or gourmet cooking.
- Plan a progressive date night in which you take turns planning the outing. For example: go dancing for her and end it with hot dogs from his favorite stand.

### TIPS FROM THE PROS
*I need girl time and couple time. So for every girl night I have with friends,
my husband and I schedule two to three date nights. It works really well for us.*
—JAMIE CAVETT, MARRIED 6 YEARS

# THE ART OF GIFT GIVING

*Love each other with genuine affection,*
*and take delight in honoring each other.*
ROMANS 12:10 NLT

## HE SAYS

Once, several weeks before an upcoming special occasion, I was excited about a gift idea for Dena. I subtly showed her the item in a catalog and asked, "How do you like this?"

She replied, "That's cute—but you're not getting me that for Christmas, are you?"

"Umm, of course not, but just out of curiosity, why wouldn't I?"

"Honey, that's a nice present, but it's not romantic."

"Okay, speak slowly, because as usual, I'm taking notes. Christmas gifts have to be *romantic*?"

"Well, sort of. I mean, a girl doesn't want her husband to get her a blender or something."

Note to self: Take back the blender.

I now know that there are slight differences between acceptable and unacceptable gifts. As in a medieval kingdom, the wife is the ruler of the land and the well-intentioned man is one of the commoners, waiting in line to offer up his basket of grain or chickens or Pandora bracelet charms to see if it appeases the queen.

So after some coaching, I think I finally understand: getting her a plain sweater is unromantic, but getting her a cashmere sweater is just lovely. Rain boots: no. But sassy paisley rain boots with a dozen roses in them? Now we're in business.

At one point in our conversation, she said, "But honey, don't you know my love language?"

"I used to, but now I think I need a translator. Somewhere along the way, your love language picked up a heavy accent or something."

Picking just the right gift can be a challenge, but she's worth it.

## SHE SAYS

I need to brag on Carey a bit. He is an excellent gift giver. Early in our marriage, we read *The Five Love Languages* (well, I read it and then summarized it for Carey, which is usually how "we" read a book) and realized that Carey's love languages were affection and quality time. My primary language, however, was gifts.

I'm sure the first time Carey realized what he was up against—we "gift" lovers feel easily slighted on special occasions and need frequent small tokens of affection to feel cherished—he might have shuddered. However, in God's wonderful providence, I married a man whose spiritual gift is giving.

Carey gets more joy out of seeing me happy than he does when I buy him a present. It's weird but true.

On the flip side, I'm an introvert with a big need for personal space. So I've had to work at giving enough affection and time to my beloved. It's not always easy, but the investment in our marriage is worth getting outside my comfort zone.

With God's help, giving to each other is something we've gotten better at over time. Also, giving to each other in the ways we feel most loved is one of the tools that keeps our union strong. Plus it makes life interesting!

*Father, You created us with such uniqueness. Help us to be creative and self-sacrificing in the ways we show love to each other.*

## TAKING OFF THE GLOVES
- Do you know your spouse's love language? Or yours? If not, find out more.
- Talk about special gifts you've given or received. What made them memorable?
- Ask your partner something that's on his or her wish list (and don't be afraid to dream big together). See if there are ways you can start praying and planning to make your spouse's wish come true (even if it takes a long, long time).

### TIPS FROM THE PROS
*Life expectations are so different now than when we were in our early married years. Honesty and common goals are essential.*
—SAMMIE CRUMP, MARRIED 56 YEARS

# LOVING EACH OTHER
# THROUGH THICK AND THIN

*Enjoy the wife you married as a young man! Lovely as an angel, beautiful as a rose—don't ever quit taking delight in her body. Never take her love for granted!*
PROVERBS 5:18–19 MSG

## HE SAYS

When Dena was pregnant with our oldest, Jordan, she didn't crave sugar or chocolate; instead, she craved salty, savory foods. I'd never been around the pregnancy block before, so I just ate when she ate. At eleven o'clock at night, Dena would say: "Honey, I really want a breakfast taquito from Whataburger." And I thought, *You know what? Me too!*

Of course, after about nine months, Dena started breathing funny one night, and eight hours later, she managed to push out her little "baby burrito bump." Unfortunately, *my* big belly stayed right where I'd put it.

So, I'd like to add another volume to the What to Expect. . . series: *What to Expect When You're Expanding–A Man's Guide to Postpartum Plumpness.* Here's a brief excerpt:

Guys, if you've been sympathy eating alongside your pregnant wife, at twenty-eight weeks, the two of you may begin to experience many of the same symptoms:
- rapid weight gain
- shortness of breath
- leg cramps
- enlargement of ankles and feet
- heartburn
- varicose veins
- the uncontrollable desire to eat food in odd combinations, such as an entire pizza topped with another pizza

Don't be alarmed; these side effects are normal for both the mom and the expanding dad. At full term, however, the results will be vastly different. Your wife will immediately lose twenty pounds over the course of one day, after she produces the cause of her ample proportions: a baby. Unfortunately for the new father, the protuberance around the midsection will take much longer to expunge. Although you will experience the desire to push and get rid of it, that won't work. However, with proper exercise (for example, running laps around Whataburger) and improved dietary habits (for example, eating only *one* sleeve of Oreos), you will notice reduced swelling over time.

## SHE SAYS

At the time, I didn't notice Carey gaining weight alongside me. I was too worried about the thirty or so pounds I had packed on (I had horrible, symptom-riddled pregnancies, and my only comfort was eating). And that was *after* losing all the baby and water weight during the first week!

Since I'm only five feet four, it doesn't take much weight for me to start to look rather. . .ahem. . .robust. But Carey was a sweetheart during and after both of my pregnancies. I can't remember him saying a word about all the weight I was putting on. He only encouraged me to take care of—and be gentle—with myself. In fact, he's loved me through thick and thin—literally. I've never moaned about my thighs or belly without him scolding me and saying, "You look beautiful. I love your body!"

Yep, he's a keeper.

I try to affirm Carey in his body-insecure moments, too. We both tend to gain weight easier now that we're older, and it truly doesn't matter to me if he's heavier than when we married. (We were just babies!) However, I do try to help him as much as I can—by shopping for and cooking healthy meals or adjusting my schedule to exercise with him.

I really don't want us to be anxious about the subject—and I don't want our kids to be, either. Our culture is strange; on the one hand, we're weight and image obsessed, and on the other, we binge eat and tip the scales until our health suffers. I think God wants us to have balance, to live life to the fullest and enjoy His good gifts in moderation.

Even yummy breakfast taquitos.

*Lord, thank You for loving us unconditionally. Give us grace for each other when we gain weight or have other changes in our appearance. Help us encourage each other and build each other up—through thick and thin.*

## TAKING OFF THE GLOVES

- Brainstorm ways to help each other stay strong and fit. Could you work out together? Maybe you could go shopping for new, exotic fruits and veggies at a farmers' market. Make a "healthy dates" list and refer to it on your weekly (or monthly) outings.

- Instead of doubting or teasing affirm your mate when he or she makes an effort to exercise, cook healthy foods, or eat better.

## TIPS FROM THE PROS

*Our motto between the two of us is "stay on the same page,"*
*so if I go walking, he tries to go walking too.*
—JAMIE CAVETT, MARRIED 6 YEARS

# THE TEXAS TWO-STEP

*Therefore encourage one another and build*
*each other up, just as in fact you are doing.*
1 THESSALONIANS 5:11

## HE SAYS

If I could go back in time and ask my single self, "What's a hobby you can see yourself picking up one day?" I'm sure the Texas two-step would be about number 308 on the list, right under Jazzercise and hanging out with cats. You see, I'm not a big country music fan, and hence, I have zero interest in country-style dancing.

And yet just last week, if you'd been at a certain party in the hill country of Texas, you'd have seen me boot-scootin' around the dance floor with my sweetheart. I'm not talking about *timid* two-step dancing, either. We did the twirls and everything! I may have even shouted, "Yee-haw!" once. You know why I did it? Because it mattered to my wife.

What makes your spouse's heart sing? The beach? Broadway musicals? Scrapbooking? (I know, hold back the gag reflex.) Men, we need to become "students" of the things our wives are passionate about. One way to express love to your wife is to take an interest in things she enjoys. I'm not saying you have to become a superfan of the ballet, hanging up *Swan Lake* posters in your wood shop. But when it comes to spending time together, make sure at least some of that time is spent talking about and doing things that "fill her tank."

Dena has always been great at reciprocating these types of gestures. For every rom-com movie we've gone to, she has accompanied me to a vocal jazz concert or a ball game. When it comes to fun activities and sharing moments together, both man and wife need to become bilingual.

## SHE SAYS

As Carey said, one way for us to care for our spouses is to do things they care about. I am a homebody, but he loves to travel. I'm also not someone who usually jumps in before I look where I'm diving. Carey, on the other hand, tends to be a "Ready-Fire-Aim!" type person. In certain areas—for example, finances and spiritual discernment—that can be dangerous, and he's learned to temper it with maturity.

But when he booked a surprise cruise for our twentieth anniversary? I didn't complain about the money he spent or moan about leaving my comfy chair and reading corner for a few days. I didn't gripe about having to get the kids or dog taken care of.

I hugged his neck, blinked back a few grateful tears, and dug out my passport. It's not every husband who will give his wife a four-day trip months before their actual anniversary, just to spoil her (and get some couple time). I'm thankful!

I haven't always been that easygoing. Here are a couple of things I've learned the hard way. Learn from me if you want to be more in tune with your mate's interests:

First, don't compete with your spouse. If you have a natural talent in a sport your sweetie likes (and you are competitive, like me), resist the urge to keep score too stringently. Instead, keep things light. Look for opportunities to laugh during your time together, and be supportive, not demeaning.

Second, set aside money to pursue your passions. If you're on a strict budget, remember to invest in the relationship. Besides money for date nights, try to funnel a few funds every now and then into special accounts (or envelopes) for travel, education, or entertainment.

A related caution: if your spouse is good at giving, then be good at receiving, even if you feel the money could be spent better another way. Say a prayer of gratitude that you have a generous mate, because so many other women (and men) are not that lucky.

*Creator God, You made my spouse with a heart that beats differently from mine. Give me a sense of adventure as I come alongside my mate. Help me be an encourager and not a discourager.*

## TAKING OFF THE GLOVES

- What passions does your partner have? Talk to each other about the things that make your heart sing.
- Brainstorm ideas about sharing in your spouse's favorite hobby— even once.
- Talk about your monthly budget. Does it include money for life-giving passions? If not, how could you adjust things so it might better reflect what you're both interested in? Be creative; there are many ways to cut costs these days.

## TIPS FROM THE PROS

*One of the most helpful things we did was meeting with a mentor couple from our church. We went once a week for several months. The accountability was very beneficial.*
—AMANDA GILBREATH, MARRIED 16 YEARS

# NOTES

# NOTES

# PART 3

# RETREATING TO OUR CORNERS

# SOCKS

## HE SAYS

Researchers say that men think about socks about twice as much as women. That statistic notwithstanding, somehow wives only want to wear socks about a tenth as much as men. When Dena actually initiates us wearing socks, I can count on one hand how many times I've refused her in twenty years. In other words, at any given moment—whether I'm healthy, sick, in a body cast, or nearly comatose—I'm up for some socks. My feet are freezing nearly all the time.

But men, your wife needs a little more ramping up before she's ready for socks. Evidently, she needs more wooing than "Hey, we've got ten minutes. You wanna?" She needs you to communicate with her throughout the day and make her feel special before she's ready to put on socks. Experts even say that doing chores around the house can get her in the mood for socks.

Our house is spotless.

One thing's for sure, though: it doesn't take much to upset the delicate balance of a woman's desire to put on socks. Whereas a man thinks wearing socks would make a headache feel better, it's just not the case for her. A female's list of "perfect socks conditions" is vastly different than a man's. She needs to feel great all over, and I mean *great*. A hangnail is enough to throw her off. She also needs to be "in the mood"—a phrase that makes absolutely no sense to a man. Do I need to be in the mood for air?

Also, in some cases, she needs Jupiter to be aligned with Mars during a leap year, in an MLB season when a Seattle Mariners right fielder makes an unassisted triple play for her to be in the mood for socks.

All things considered, the sometimes confusing game of socks keeps things interesting. And let's face it—wearing socks with the one you love is awesome, so don't get cold feet.

## SHE SAYS

Speaking of cold feet—one of the issues for me in wearing socks was the way I was brought up. In my family of origin, the word *socks* was not uttered. I was not allowed to watch television or movies that alluded to socks. In my church youth group, I was taught socks were dangerous. At summer camp, the preacher said that to please God and be a "good girl," you went barefoot all the way up to the honeymoon. While that is God's ideal, it had the unintended effect of making me feel guilty about even thinking about socks when my hormones starting raging.

I don't begrudge the lack of socks education I received; it just made me more thankful I found *Preparing for Adolescence* in my church library. Dr. James Dobson gave me helpful information about socks from a biblical perspective.

I do know this: with God's help and a patient spouse, wearing socks as a couple just gets better as the years go by. You can wear a better variety of socks, and you know what kinds of socks make your spouse happy. It's yet another way God weaves the hearts of men and women together.

And it's darn fun.

*God, thank You for giving us the gift of intimacy—in all its forms. We love Your creativity and the way You created a man's body for a woman's, and vice versa. Forgive us when we withhold ourselves for selfish reasons, and give us patience and an attitude of self-sacrifice when we can't be together. Help us to honor each other and keep finding ways to connect our mind, souls, and bodies.*

## TAKING OFF THE GLOVES

- Are both of you satisfied with the frequency of and variety in your sex life? If not, talk honestly and gently about the ways you could make changes.

- If you need to, enlist the help of a trained Christian counselor. A counselor can be instrumental in finding (and helping heal) deep wounds, negative thinking patterns, and harmful behavior cycles. Many of them charge on a sliding scale based on income, and some will take insurance.

- Try to get away together for a weekend (or at least a night) once or twice a year—without the kids. It will do wonders for your attitude and can lead to some wonderful intimacy! If your budget is tight, consider trading child care with another couple or ask family members to help out. You could even "swap" houses with someone local who wants to have a cheap getaway without the costs associated with hotels, taxis, flights, etc.

## TIPS FROM THE PROS
*Be honest. Honesty leads to wisdom.*
—GAIL HAYES, MARRIED 31 YEARS

# TO LOVE AND TO CHERISH
## (PART 1)

*Two are better than one, because they have a good return for their
labor: If either of them falls down, one can help the other up.
But pity anyone who falls and has no one to help them up.*
ECCLESIASTES 4:9–10

## HE SAYS

". . .to love and to cherish." I'm not an expert at semantics (which
hopefully isn't evident in this book). So when I said "to love and to cherish"
in front of God and all the others who fit inside First Baptist Church,
Dumas, Texas, on that Saturday, July 8, 1995, I thought those two words
were basically synonymous. Love = cherish. Right?

The word *love* is perhaps the best example of how the English language
falls short. Our culture has kidnapped this word and tried to make it both
meaningful and nonchalant. "I love my mom. I love this latte. I love *The
Princess Bride*." To quote Inigo Montoya, "You keep using that word. I do not
think it means what you think it means."

The Greeks got it right. They have at least three or four separate ways of
expressing the word *love*. The first one is *eros*. This is love based on physical
attraction and desire. I guess Dena was first attracted to me because she had
a thing for short guys who still live with their parents.

*Phileo* is a brotherly or sisterly love that comes out of bonding. This is
the kind of love that many women have for their. . .chocolate. (Side note: I
always wondered if *phileo* was the phonetic inspiration for the Filet-O-Fish
sandwich. Probably not. I've never really bonded with one.)

By far the best of the Greek loves is *agape*. This is a supernatural love—a
love that can be experienced only through Christ.

You'll experience the full range of Greek love in your marriage
relationship. When my sweetie smiles and wrinkles up her nose in a way she
is probably unaware of, I am *eros*-ing the bejeebies out of her.

When we just sit in the quiet, talk, and bear each other's burdens after
the kids are in bed, our *phileo* love makes an appearance. And the deep,
abiding love that bonds us together as Christ's kinsmen? That's *agape*. God
is both the foundation and the glue, if you will, that holds it all together.

## SHE SAYS

God *is* the glue. There is no way I can be the wife my husband needs me to be without His help. After all, sometimes I don't feel *eros* love for Carey. Sometimes I don't even feel very *phileo* about him (especially when he leads the boys in a belching contest).

However, because the Holy Spirit resides in me, I can make a choice to love Carey regardless of my emotions. I can pray for help to put down the fleshly/sinful part of me and—instead of listening to what it wants—lay it on the altar. That's when *agape* love takes over.

Author Jennifer Kennedy Dean calls such moments "altar'd" moments.[2] These are small crucifixions when we choose to lay down our flesh. In doing so, we free the Spirit to transform us even further into the likeness of Christ. The best part? New life is sure to follow.

And when Christ loves our spouse through us—that, my friends, is a very good thing.

*Holy Spirit, thank You for Your presence and activity in our marriage.*
*Move among us. Remind us of the help that is so readily available to us.*
*Convict us of sin, and give us strength to choose to love our mate,*
*especially when we don't "feel" very loving. May we see many resurrection*
*moments as we grow closer to You and each other.*

## TAKING OFF THE GLOVES
- Talk about moments when you've experienced the different kinds of love (*eros*, *phileo*, *agape*). What function does each kind of love serve in your relationship?
- What do you think "new life" means in regard to marriage; have you seen any of those in your marriage?
- Pray together, inviting the Holy Spirit to be more active in your union and to transform you more fully into Jesus' likeness.

---

2. *Jennifer Kennedy Dean, Altar'd: Experience the Power of Resurrection* (New Hope Publishers, 2012)

## TIPS FROM THE PROS

*At this stage of our married life, cherishing each other looks like blocking out distractions—kids, social media, busy schedules; carving out little moments to hug him good-bye or kiss him hello; listening with full attention. It's making the effort not to take each other for granted. Sometimes it's best seen when we stop to remember our whole love story, laugh, and be thankful for it all.*

—HEATHER ENRIGHT, MARRIED 20 YEARS

# TO LOVE AND TO CHERISH
## (PART 2)

*Though one may be overpowered, two can defend themselves.*
*A cord of three strands is not quickly broken.*
ECCLESIASTES 4:12

## HE SAYS

"...to love and to cherish." Cherish? Like I said, I didn't really understand what the word meant when I uttered my vows twenty pounds ago.

I did know that "Cherish" was the title of a song released by Madonna during the summer after my senior year. The black-and-white music video featured her rolling around in the sand on a beach while occasionally frolicking around with three mermen. However, since neither Madonna's lyrics nor grayscale, mythical aquatics are exactly hailed as bastions of information on marital purity, I had to look elsewhere for understanding.

Luckily, a few years of marital mileage helped me realize in retrospect just what I was pledging when I said "cherish."

I have an old 1960s Sears and Roebuck radio in my office. It still works, and it belonged to my grandparents. Whenever I visited them, it was always there in their home, and for me, it has come to represent the musical heritage passed down in my family. I hold this radio very dear to my heart, I protect it, and I'm "softened" whenever I look at it. I've always enjoyed listening to the radio in my car, too, but I could care less about the radio itself. However, I *cherish* my grandparents' radio.

Our spouses should feel cherished. While "love" describes the powerful affection that God gives two people for each other, the word *cherish* brings to mind being treasured, deeply cared for, safe, and feeling at home with someone. My wife should feel as if she's on a pedestal—not in a boastful or idolatrous way, but because she's special and deserving of my admiration. She should be completely at ease and unintimidated by her place in my life and in the intimacy we share.

She should feel cherished.

## SHE SAYS

Likewise, a man should feel cherished by his wife. An important question to ask early on in your relationship is, "What makes you feel cherished?" Ask for specific ideas about how to show your spouse love in practical, daily ways.

As we've noted previously, when we were first married, we read *The Five Love Languages* by Gary Chapman. Since then, we've used the principles many times.

I can't recommend this resource highly enough. In the book, Chapman explains the five love "personalities" and notes that we often long to receive love in different ways than how our spouse wants to receive it. It's such a simple—okay, brilliant—way to describe the vastly separate desires men and women have. (Add in disparate personality types and temperaments, and it's a wonder any of us stay married at all!)

For instance, Carey feels treasured by me when I spend time with him—walking and talking, going on a dinner and movie date, or just sitting with him and watching a television show while holding hands. On the other hand, I feel deeply cared for when he brings me gifts. They don't have to be large; in fact, small gifts (a magazine he thinks I'd like or a small bouquet of fresh flowers from the grocery store) are just as meaningful to me, because it shows me that he's been thinking about me.

Cherish your spouse. It's the simplest—and most long-lasting—investment you can make in your marriage.

*Jesus, You showed us how to cherish each other by the ways You've loved us. You served in humility, washed Your disciples' feet, and even sacrificed to the point of death. Help us deeply value and treasure our mates so that they feel safe with us, just as we feel safe with You.*

## TAKING OFF THE GLOVES

- If you haven't asked before, ask your spouse now, "How do you feel cherished? What specific ways could I show you that I deeply value and esteem you?"
- Talk about the times each of you has felt treasured in your relationship. What action, word, or attitude from your spouse made you feel that way?
- Write down ideas about dates you could plan in which you take turns cherishing the other person in specific ways.

## TIPS FROM THE PROS

*When Casey goes to bed before me, he leaves the master bath light on and the door cracked so I can find my way to my side of the bed. This is so endearing to me. It's small, but it makes me feel loved.*
—MISTY DUMAS, MARRIED 14 YEARS

# COLOR BLIND

*For we walk by faith, not by sight.*
2 CORINTHIANS 5:7 NASB

## SHE SAYS

When Carey and I first met, I was drawn to many things about him. His heart for God was superattractive; his clothes, not so much.

I have photos from the first few years of knowing my hubby that could be fodder for blackmail in future years. (I'll never tell where they are.) Suffice it to say, my love for him blossomed while my concern about his obvious deficit in fashion also grew.

It wasn't until he had an eye exam in his late thirties that we discovered he had an actual condition. This malady causes him to not see colors correctly. *I knew it!*

We now have a very firm rule in the Dyer house: Carey does not go shopping without me. We've learned the hard way that any solo trip to the mall will result in a pile of clothes that don't go together. (They do to him, but in reality they clash.)

It's a good thing that early on he learned to trust me implicitly. Either that, or he's tired of wasting money on clothes he can't wear.

And you know what? It's really not a big deal. After all, he's blind to many of my faults, so I'll take his color-challenged fashion sense any day.

## HE SAYS

I don't "suffer" from my own color blindness. I'm quite fine with it, actually. However, Dena has suffered from my color blindness for years—mostly by having to be seen with me in public after I've dressed myself.

I have what doctors refer to as red/green deficiency. I'm not good at distinguishing between different shades of certain colors (for me, some reds, blues, and purples). Incidentally, I have researched enough to know that cows are also red/green color blind. Unfortunately, this similarity between me and my bovine brethren has not prevented me from regularly partaking of copious amounts of red meat—at least, I *think* it was red.

In college I would occasionally get around this confusion by wearing the same color pants and shirt. I reasoned, "If it's the exact same, then I *know* it matches." Such thinking resulted in me looking like a toddler wearing a 1980s Garanimals "outfit." The culmination of my short-lived, monochromatic style was the day that I wore all light brown. I entered the cafeteria to confidence-boosting howls of "Here comes the UPS man!" (a nickname that lasted longer than I like to admit).

And now that I'm a quasi-adult, the prelude to certain date nights finds me sitting on the edge of the bed, half dressed and patiently waiting for my wife to come out of the bathroom so I can ask her like a five-year-old, "Does this match?"

"No, sweetie," she says, kindly leaving off "bless your heart."

Dena helps me. She's quite good at color coordinating her inept hubby's clothes. Even in something as silly as my hang-ups with hues, the Lord put us together to fill in each other's gaps.

It's like the oh-so-wise philosopher Rocky Balboa says: "You's got gaps and I's got gaps, but together we ain't got no gaps."

Certainly, as Christians our wholeness and identity is found in Christ alone. However, I'm also certain that one reason my mate and I became one flesh was to strengthen each other as individuals.

I am a stronger me with her.

*Jesus, You complete us as individuals, and in Your perfect plan, we complement each other as a couple. Thank You for giving us a mate whose strengths fill in the gaps left by our weaknesses. And help us be blind to each other's faults when we need to be—instead, seeing our mates as You see them. Let us walk by faith in You, and not only by what we see with our eyes.*

## TAKING OFF THE GLOVES

- Have you ever taken time to thank your spouse for the small—and big—ways he or she helps you? Do that now.
- In what areas could you be "blind" to something your spouse is not? Do you leave things around the house instead of picking them up? Do you continually ignore an area that is causing your mate distress? Pray and ask God to open your eyes.
- Look back through pictures of the two of you in different decades and laugh together at the clothing and hairstyles you wore.

## TIPS FROM THE PROS

*Give away all the love, mercy, and grace you can muster
(even when it's hard!). When each of you does that,
you each automatically receive lots of love, mercy, and grace.*
—SANDRA TATE, MARRIED 41 YEARS

# WHEN OPPOSITES PARENT TOGETHER

*God-loyal people, living honest lives,*
*make it much easier for their children.*
PROVERBS 20:7 MSG

## HE SAYS

A winter morning when a typical clueless dad is in charge:

"Kids! Up and at 'em! Your ride's leaving in ten minutes! Here, take this frozen waffle with you—you can heat it with the car's defrost setting. Clean towels? Where do you think we live, the Marriott? Oh, sorry, son, I lost your medical release form for the field trip. Just tell Mrs. Carr to text me which hospital to come to if there's a problem."

(At this point, the youngest child emerges from his room, dressed in a flannel shirt, shorts, and flip-flops while wielding some sort of makeshift weapon.)

"Hey, mister, you're not leaving the house dressed like that! Go put on a hat!"

In contrast, here's a likely scenario when Supermom—also known as the hummingbird, because of her capacity for hovering—is in charge:

"Angel darling? Up and at 'em! I'll be in to bathe you in just a minute; got to be clean as a whistle for your first day of eighth grade. The carpool will be here at 7:32. This is Mrs. Morton's week to drive, so I've put a small cranberry candle in your backpack as a thank-you gift. I'm packing your lunch today. I shelled some organic edamame pods and ground some fresh lemon zest for your Kona water. I also put two copies of your signed medical release form in your amethyst folder, plus I e-mailed one to the school and another to the curator of the museum you'll be touring. Oh, and I pinned a reminder note on your jacket with our family word of the month: *excel*!"

Of course, the above examples are the extreme opposite ends of the spectrum, and most of us fall somewhere in the middle. Fortunately, just as seemingly incompatible personalities can work in a marriage relationship, different parenting styles can ideally "meet in the middle" to complement each other quite nicely.

## SHE SAYS

If you play these different personalities right, you can parent like "good cop, bad cop" and your child will be none the wiser.

> *Scene: living room in a typical suburban house. A mother and father are standing by the coffee table while a sullen teenager sits on the sofa.*
>
> Mom: Honey, I know you were out with friends, but you still have to call if you're going to be late.
>
> Teen: I told you a hundred times—I was caught in traffic!
>
> Dad: Don't speak to your mother that way. Look at me when I'm talking to you! Do you understand that we were worried sick?
>
> Teen: Well, *I'm* sick of you not trusting me!
>
> Dad: Trust is earned. It's a privilege, not a *right*. And don't look at me that way!
>
> Mom: What your dad is trying to say is that we would appreciate it if you'd think about how we don't sleep when you're gone. And a simple phone call will help keep us sane.

In all sincerity, Carey and I have learned that God's design for our marriage extends to parenting. When we keep communication lines open between the two of us and divide up responsibilities according to our personalities and gifts, things go much smoother.

If our ultimate goal is not to raise perfect kids (because that's impossible) but to launch young adults who have God's kingdom as their priority, we can stand united in purpose and keep our perspective, our sense of humor—and our sanity!

> *Lord, parenting is difficult, even on the best of days. We thank You for the gift of children, and we ask for Your wisdom and discernment to parent them in godly, Spirit-led ways. Help us communicate well and not let our children divide us. Instead, may we be united in purpose and grateful for the privilege of raising kingdom-minded kids.*

## TAKING OFF THE GLOVES

- How have your different parenting styles caused conflict?
- How have your parenting styles been complementary?
- How could you communicate better in regard to parenting?

## TIPS FROM THE PROS

*When I married Mike, it was a second marriage for both of us. Each of us had a daughter—both born in 1970. Our main goal was to give the girls good role models, especially about how a loving Christian marriage looks and sounds.*
—Janie Simms, married 37 years

# TRANSLATION, PLEASE

*A word fitly spoken is like apples of gold in a setting of silver.*
PROVERBS 25:11 ESV

## HE SAYS

"Let's not worry about it. We'll celebrate it later this year." That's pretty much what Dena said regarding our fifth anniversary. We both had to work all day on the momentous occasion, so we agreed to wait a bit until we had time to savor it together.

Unfortunately, with this cursed male brain of mine, I took Dena's words literally. I truly didn't think about it that day. No card, no verbal acknowledgment, no sticky note on her mirror. I basically acted like our anniversary didn't exist. (Cue the *Jaws* theme music.) That didn't go over too well.

> Me: But I thought you said we weren't going to celebrate it today!
>
> Her: Well, you could've at least gotten me a card or *something*!

To this day, it's the one anniversary that I really screwed up. I guess one out of twenty-one ain't bad (or is it twenty-two?).

Sometimes I wish wives came equipped with a button similar to the "Google translate" feature on my laptop. We'll call it the "Google trans-mate" app. That way, when a wife says something confusing, the husband can pause the moment, check the translation, and then respond accordingly.

> Her: Let's not worry about it. We'll celebrate it later this year.
>
> Trans-mate: We may not have time to go on a date or anything, but if you don't at least kiss me or give me some flowers or *something*, you can expect to find the severed head of a large teddy bear in your bed the next morning.
>
> Her: Honey, how does this dress look on me?

Trans-mate: Look, we both know that I gained five pounds last weekend. How was I to know that Beth's baby shower would include a chocolate fountain with a selection of fruits and sponge cakes? And yes, I may or may not have put my quiche under the fountain when no one was looking. But if you value the next five minutes of your life and want to avoid a stare that could melt a Hummer, you'd better tell me that I look good.

## SHE SAYS

I like that idea! Google Trans-mate could help wives, too:

Him: Fine.
Trans-mate: Actually, work was hard today. Like, brutal! I just want to sit here in my boxers and watch the game—while eating copious amounts of chips—without anyone bothering me for a couple of hours, and then I can get back to the work of being a husband.

Him: Want to?
Trans-mate: I miss you so much. We're apart all day, and when I see you, you are so beautiful that all I want to do is take you in my arms, kiss you until you can't breathe, and make you happier than you've ever been.

Him: Okay.
Trans-mate: I didn't really hear you, but in my heart of hearts, I want to help you with the housework and the kids. I just have a million things on my mind. So if you'll write your request down on a list and remind me about it, I promise I'll complete it—at least in the next six months.

So Google folks, if you're listening—I think we have a million-dollar idea here. Get on it!

*So often we misunderstand each other. We jump to conclusions, say the*
*wrong things, and frustrate each other. Help us be better listeners, Lord.*
*Give us grace for the times we mishear and misinterpret our loved one's*
*words or intentions. And thank You for Your forgiveness when we misstep.*

## TAKING OFF THE GLOVES

- What is something you wish you had known about communication when you were dating or first married?
- Talk about a time when one of you totally misunderstood the other.
- Are you holding on to a grudge or hurt feelings due to miscommunication? Ask for forgiveness from God and each other.
- Think about technological advances that could help your union. Have fun and be silly together!

## TIPS FROM THE PROS

*Take time daily to connect in undivided conversation about your day.*
*Give each other time to pursue your own hobbies/interests. . . .*
*And intentionally work to find shared activities—this involves compromise.*
—HEATHER ENRIGHT, MARRIED 20 YEARS

# IN SICKNESS AND IN HEALTH
## (PART 1)

*Now that we know what we have—Jesus, this great High Priest with ready*
*access to God—let's not let it slip through our fingers. We don't have a priest*
*who is out of touch with our reality. He's been through weakness and testing,*
*experienced it all—all but the sin. So let's walk right up to him and get*
*what he is so ready to give. Take the mercy, accept the help.*
HEBREWS 4:14–16 MSG

## HE SAYS

". . .in sickness and in health." You have no real way of knowing exactly what you're pledging before God and your wedding guests when you utter those five little words. But like every other part of your vows, this phrase will be tested.

Here's the thing I didn't realize. If you study the entire vow sentence, what you're really agreeing to is "to have and to hold" in all of these situations. Having and holding in health is pretty easy, but. . .in sickness? Holding? Really?

It was around our second or third Valentine's Day as a married couple. We went to a little Italian restaurant that had sponge-painted walls, which gives you an idea of how fancy the place wasn't and how much money we didn't have. Dena ordered the cheapest thing on the menu—so cheap, in fact, that it contained traces of salmonella (which I believe goes best with a red wine). Our romantic evening ended with Dena's head in what the Italians call a *gabinetto*. Turns out that my job that night was "to have and to hold" her hair back while she called Ralph on the porcelain phone.

Dena's had her share of "in sickness" moments with me, too. Confession is good for the soul, right? I'm kind of a wimp when I'm sick. Some guys like to keep going and not slow down when they're ill, just work through the pain. Not me. . .at all. Sure, when I'm well I like to come off as the man of the house as much as the next somewhat virile male, but give me a smidgen of fever and some mild body aches, and I'm on a pallet on the couch like a four-year-old, calling out to my wife in a whiny voice to bring me more Sprite in "that cup that I like."

Whether it's me staying up with Dena while she's yodeling groceries, or her having to put up with an ailing hubby who has all the courage of a puppy, guess what? It's what we signed up for, and we don't mind it one bit. True love and commitment can make you do crazy things, even if you find yourself in the middle of a mess.

## SHE SAYS

To be honest, Carey has had to lean into this part of our vows more than I would have liked. In our twenty-year union, I've been diagnosed with Hashimoto's—an autoimmune thyroid disease—and degenerative disk disease stemming from genetics and a car wreck in college (leading to neck fusion surgery). I've also dealt with two very tough pregnancies, postpartum depression, and various female issues. Since we are a team, he had to deal with the fallout from my problems, as well as shoulder the familial burden (physically, emotionally, and financially) when I couldn't.

It's not what he expected—but he has taken it (mostly) in stride. And when he's ill, I impart love, mercy, and chicken soup to him.

When our spouses are sick, it's important that we do whatever we can to lessen their load and make them feel cared for. By cooking or buying takeout, helping with household chores and the boys' homework, and holding me when I cry or hurt, Carey has shown his love to me and lived out his vow to cherish me "in sickness and in health." He's taken me to doctor visits, fetched medicines, paid for massages, and whisked me away for much-needed retreats. Sometimes he takes the boys to do fun guy things so I can have a quiet house for reading, writing, or resting.

Sure, "having and holding" is easier when things are going well, but the moments in marriage that define us as a couple—and can ultimately bring us closer to God and each other—are those in which we have and hold, no matter how hard it is.

And truly? There's nothing more romantic than a man who will spend Valentine's Day taking care of you when you're sick.

*Jehovah Rapha, You are the God who heals. Thank You for giving us each other, and please give us grace and strength when one or both of us face illness.*

## TAKING OFF THE GLOVES
- What makes you feel better when you're sick? Be honest!
- Talk about ways to meet each other's needs the next time illness happens.

- Thank your spouse for the ways he or she has helped you during sickness.

## TIPS FROM THE PROS

*We went through a lot of rough times, including my husband's fourteen major illnesses (he took a medical retirement at forty-eight after a heart attack and Crohn's disease, suffered from arthritis since the third grade, and passed away this last March). What kept us going, besides prayer, was humor. We managed to see the funny side of a lot of things.*

—DONNA GOODRICH, A WIDOW AFTER BEING MARRIED 55 YEARS

# IN SICKNESS AND IN HEALTH
## (PART 2)

*Love never gives up, never loses faith, is always hopeful,*
*and endures through every circumstance.*
1 Corinthians 13:7 NLT

## SHE SAYS

It took time for Carey to understand I wasn't making up the fatigue I felt when we were first married. His family grew up as healthy as pack mules (they went to the pharmacist instead of the doctor on the rare occasion one of them felt sick) while my bout with severe mononucleosis during our engagement began a downhill slide with my health. It left me tired all the time and seeking medical help from multiple doctors and specialists. I've simply never felt the same as I did before that lengthy illness.

At times I've cried hot tears of frustration because I am not as energetic as I'd like. "I wish I were stronger," I said to Carey more than once when my body betrayed me—again. He's sweet and understanding, but I know that it can be hard for him, as well. I've also been mad at God more than once for not snapping His fingers and healing me in one fell swoop, as I know He could. The problems I have been saddled with have no immediate cure, at least not yet.

However, I'm thankful for God's strength in my weakness. I'm also grateful for good food, the right medicine, caring doctors, and exercise, which have all helped me immensely. Carey has also given me a huge gift by learning how to listen to me, support me, and help me in practical ways.

## HE SAYS

I can't relate firsthand to what it's been like to experience Dena's debilitating symptoms, but I have learned my fair share of what to do—and maybe more importantly what not to do—as the spouse of someone who is suffering. If you have a sick spouse, especially when that illness is prolonged, perhaps what I've learned will encourage you.

1. *Don't be dismissive.* I usually have fuel to spare, and Dena has spent much of our time together just trying to keep up. Early in our marriage, I thought Dena should be able to "shake it off" when she felt ill, as if her symptoms were something she could turn off and on at will. I was

unknowingly making her feel "less than," like she didn't have what it took to make me happy. I learned that my slowing down and trying to be more understanding was good for what ailed her.

2. *Do be sensitive.* This probably goes without saying. However, looking back on times that Dena dealt with her illness for months and even years on end, sometimes I would (dare I say it?) get used to it. I forgot that she was physically and emotionally dealing with pain or fatigue day in and day out. In my busyness, sometimes days would go by before I acknowledged what she was going through. In my more sensitive moments, an extended hug, a knowing glance, or a quick text let her know that I cared and wanted to go through this with her.

3. *Don't forget the simple things.* Never underestimate the power of a cup of fresh-brewed coffee waiting for her when she wakes, or the simple act of getting up fifteen minutes earlier so that she doesn't have a pile of dishes greeting her first thing in the morning. I discovered that anything, whether great or small, that I could do to bear Dena's burden went a long way in keeping her on the path to wellness.

4. *Do pray.* It's just like the Lord to take something that is difficult and turn it into an opportunity to grow closer in your relationship as man and wife. We haven't ever had a quiet, candlelit house full of Billy Graham–style, inspired intercession. But there have been moments I've sidled up to Dena, kissed her on the cheek, and begun praying for her, unannounced. Other times, while tucking the boys in for the night, I've asked, "How about we pray for Mommy?"

Finally, know that God never leaves us for a second. While He may (or may not) heal our loved one here on earth, He *is* always working to transform us into His image. In the midst of the trial, be deliberate about fixing your eyes on Jesus and leaving room for supernatural intervention.

*Abba Father, it's hard to keep our eyes on You when one of us suffers. Help us focus our gaze on You when life becomes difficult and our road is steep. When our spouse hurts, nudge us to respond in loving-kindness. When we hurt, remind us that You hurt with us. We trust You to bring beauty from the ashes of illness and disease. Bring us closer together through our pain and our spouse's pain.*

## TAKING OFF THE GLOVES

- Does one of you get sick more often than the other? Talk about how that affects you both.
- Discuss ways to support each other if and when illness descends on your marriage.
- Decide together to implement one (or more) of Carey's action steps if you haven't already done so.

## TIPS FROM THE PROS

*We are always each other's advocate, whether in a doctor's office or hospital. It's comforting to know someone is listening, asking questions, and taking notes.*
—CAROL WELSTEAD, MARRIED 33 YEARS

# TWO SCOOPS O' CRAZY

*"Peace I leave with you; My peace I give to you;*
*not as the world gives do I give to you.*
*Do not let your heart be troubled, nor let it be fearful."*
JOHN 14:27 NASB

## SHE SAYS

Carey is the stricter parent, while I'm more lenient. At times the boys try to manipulate the situation—with warlike strategy and crafty precision. I imagine it goes something like this:

"She's tired tonight. Let's hit her up for extra allowance before Dad gets home," says my oldest ("The General").

"Good idea," replies my youngest ("The Private"). "I'll go soften her up by cuddling on the couch and holding her hand. She likes that because I'm pulling away as I journey through adolescence."

"Perfect! When I come in, you kiss her on the cheek—that will be the fatal blow—and then I'll make our case."

Sometimes I cave. However, I try to stay strong, at least until my reinforcement arrives. Then Carey and I present a united front.

Take, for instance, the time when one of the children got upset at me for (horror of horrors!) making them ride with someone else to their fine arts academy—because I'd just had neck fusion surgery and was forbidden from driving in traffic.

"I want to be adopted by another family!" my son cried before getting in the other person's vehicle.

I called Carey, venting about how this child was being overdramatic and selfish. "He wants to be adopted out, and I'm thinking we should agree," I said.

I knew, once again, that God had given me the right spouse, because the love of my life calmly replied, "That's fine with me. Just make sure he knows he'll have to pay for the legal fees."

## HE SAYS

We live in an artsy, passionate family with energy to spare. So, as you can imagine, sometimes our home can be "two scoops o' crazy with a side of koo-koo-kachoo."

Once when the boys were little toddler monkeys, all four of us were at home, sick with various illnesses involving some type of phlegm. As a matter of fact, we were collectively hyped up on so many meds, it's no wonder what happened next.

After being cooped up in the house all day, our sons decided to run around the house with their shirts off, screaming gibberish at the top of their lungs like rabid ferrets. Of course, the younger one got hurt somehow and began crying.

As Mommy Dyer tried to wrangle the now-fighting boys (which, at this point, was like trying to nail Jell-O to the wall), how did Daddy Dyer respond: Join the fray? Grab my Bible or pray?

Nope. I headed for the powdered donuts for a little stress eating. With each increasing decibel from the kids, I consumed another white donut. One donut, two donuts, three. . . The cacophony of screaming children, buzz-saw eating, and throat-clearing coughs reached a fever pitch. Eventually, no one could see through the white-powdered haze hovering over our kitchen like a British fog.

Not the best way to handle a tough situation, was it? Before He died and rose again, Jesus said He was leaving us with a gift—peace of mind and heart. However, some days I forget to open that gift, and things get. . .intense.

You see, the peace of God is a gift, but a gift is not truly a gift until it is received.

*Lord, let us not forget to go to You when our lives get crazy.*
*Forgive us for trying to handle stressful situations on our own.*
*Give us strength not to run toward worldly comforts and solutions.*
*Instead, remind us to focus on Your peace and receive it as the gift it is.*

## TAKING OFF THE GLOVES

- What are some of the best—and worst—times you've shared as parents?
- In what ways do you seek God's peace in the midst of chaos? How could you remind yourself to open the gift of peace He is eager to give?
- Ask your spouse for his or her perspective on this. Your spouse may be able to offer some advice about ways you could avoid getting swept up into life's hurricane.

## TIPS FROM THE PROS

*We dated once a week at Subway after our then-youngest got dropped off at preschool. We shared a six-inch sandwich, drank water, and talked—and not about the kids. We started to remember what it was that first attracted us to each other!*
—SANDY MCKEOWN, MARRIED 36 YEARS

# TRY A LITTLE ROMANCE

*My beloved speaks and says to me:*
*"Arise, my love, my beautiful one, and come away."*
SONG OF SONGS 2:10 ESV

## HE SAYS

In my younger days, I used to sing oldies rock 'n' roll at a couple of different music theaters. Once when I was crooning the Platters classic "Only You," a seventy-something-year-old gentleman in the front row reached over and gently took the hand of his sweetheart—the same as he had surely done when that song played on the jukebox during their teenage years.

Guys, I can't point to a specific Bible verse that says, "Be thou romantic," although the entire book of Song of Songs (sometimes call the Song of Solomon) is a good place to start. However, adding a dose of true, old-fashioned, gushy romance into your marriage is at *least* a noble idea and at *most* a relationship-transforming gesture.

Too many of us say, "Well, that's just not me." I'm afraid in the name of not wanting to appear soft, we're missing out on an opportunity for deeper intimacy with our spouses. Remember, marriage (and life, for that matter) is not simply about what you can get out of it but what you can give to it. Here are a couple of reminders for the romantically faint of heart:

1. *It doesn't take much.* You don't have to don a suit of armor while quoting an original sonnet and revealing the wrinkled ticket you saved from your first movie together. Simply doing something *just for her* is what matters to most women. A note that says, "Thinking about you at work today," placed by her coffeemaker in the morning is enough to do the trick. Turns out, it truly is the thought that counts.

2. *It doesn't make you less of a man.* Being committed to one woman and letting her know it on a regular basis, even at the risk of "playing the fool"—*that's* being a man. And let me just shoot straight with you: wooing your wife with a bit of romance usually gets her engine running, if you know what I mean.

3. *Romance blesses your wife.* Now I know that somewhere in the world there may be a woman who isn't into such acts of adoration. But in all my years, I've rarely met a woman who didn't enjoy a fresh bouquet of

"just-because flowers" or a tasteful compliment on how she looks. At the end of the day, it's not really about a husband's comfort level with romance. We do it for her.

God designed our wives to respond to romance. Whether you have a dynamite marriage or need help finding your way back to each other, showing your spouse that you're still head-over-heels in love is a step in the right direction.

## SHE SAYS

I am thankful to have a husband who knows that romance is essential to keeping a marriage strong.

Did you know that the Bible is full of romance? I'm not just talking about Song of Songs, either. The scriptures tell an overarching story of God romancing His people, providing for them, and giving them everything their hearts could desire in His kingdom. Jesus called the church His bride, and Paul encouraged husbands to love their wives as Christ loves the church.

Ladies, our men may not have the same need for romance as we do (though some of them are just as much suckers for sappy movies or cards as we are), but when we love our spouses, we are fulfilling God's command to love others as we love ourselves.

Self-sacrificing relationships teach us more about God because He is the author of love. He created us for deep intimacy, and He often uses our familial bonds to share lessons about His own love for us.

So try a little romance, and watch for the myriad ways God shows His love for you.

*Father, You are the divine romancer. Throughout the Bible, You showed us the way to unconditional, passionate, self-sacrificial love. Give us boldness to romance our spouses. Help us not take each other for granted but instead keep making an effort to show our lovers how much they mean to us.*

## TAKING OFF THE GLOVES

- Ask your partner about specific romantic gestures they appreciate. Try to incorporate more of these into your marriage.
- Ladies, ask your husband about romantic ideas (dinner at a nice restaurant, flirty text messages, or a night away from the kids) you can implement for him, too!

- Read the biblical book Song of Songs together over several nights. Find a biblical commentary to read alongside it, if you'd like.

## TIPS FROM THE PROS

*My husband sends me sweet texts throughout the day. He knows I can never hear "I love you" too much. I try to cherish him by keeping the house as uncluttered as possible, doing little chores, and making things he likes for dinner.*
—REBECCA CARRELL, MARRIED 11 YEARS

# NOTES

# NOTES

# PART 4

# NEEDING A REFEREE

# THE LOW POINT
# (PART 1)

*"So do not fear, for I am with you; do not be dismayed, for I am your God. I will strengthen you and help you; I will uphold you with my righteous right hand."*
ISAIAH 41:10

## SHE SAYS

A few years ago, we went through one of the most emotionally draining and spiritually challenging times in our relationship. It was harrowing, to tell you the truth.

Months passed without a break in the clouds, and I cried out to God for relief. He encouraged me through scripture and songs, friends and family members. However, the rain continued falling, and the ground beneath me seemed to crumble.

I wasn't sure if we would make it out of the darkness together. There were moments when I said to myself, *This is how people split up*. (I'd never thought that before.)

But I'm going to let Carey tell you about this period in our marriage because it started with a job change and got worse—much worse.

## HE SAYS

It was one of the true low points in my life. In a matter of months, I had gone from a decent-paying job I loved to serving frozen yogurt and substitute teaching—anything I could find to pay the bills. To say it was a humbling experience is an understatement.

In addition, I had just turned forty, so I began to emotionally cave under something that I thought just happened to "other guys": the midlife crisis. We had to move from a house to a much smaller apartment in a town I didn't like. I could go on, but you get the picture. It didn't take long for the classic symptoms to kick in: weight gain, days of not wanting to get out of bed, alienating myself from friends and family.

Happy-go-lucky Carey—the life of the party—was in the throes of depression.

As I look back on that time now, the most surprising part of it all is this: I thought I was okay. "Just going through a rough spot," I'd tell myself, male pride intact. "Sure, I'm kind of down, and maybe Dena and I are arguing a bit more than usual, but I'll bounce back."

However, it's hard to bounce back when the ball is deflated. I needed help.

With the prayerful support of my sweet bride, who had to put up with a lot of "stuff" (for lack of a better term), I eventually got the help I needed. It involved a combination of physical, emotional, and spiritual changes in my life, many of them *way* out of my comfort zone. But here's the thing: it was worth it. A happier family, a healthier life, drawing closer to my Lord— those things were worth coming face-to-face with the uglier parts of myself.

So, I want to encourage all of my male readers who may be experiencing something similar or even more serious. Here's a bit of sincere, I've-been-there-before, tough love: Get over your machismo. Humble yourself before the Lord, before your spouse and kids, before a friend, counselor, or pastor— and get the help you need. Your well-being and your family are worth it. Otherwise, you may look up someday to find that your male pride is about all you have left.

*Father, give us the humility and strength to seek help when we
need it. Thank You for medicines, physicians, counselors, friends,
and loved ones who reach out their arms to us when we are falling.
Let us bear their burdens when they struggle, too.*

## TAKING OFF THE GLOVES
- Have either of you struggled with depression?
- If you have, and you're on the other side of it, talk about some of the ways you found hope and healing.
- If you're in the midst of depression's insidious grip, talk honestly about ways to heal. Pray together about it if both of you are willing.

## TIPS FROM THE PROS
*We are just there for each other. If I need to talk, he listens.
If he needs to be quiet and process his thoughts, I sit and hold his hand.
But the most important thing is we pray for each other.*
—IDA RICHARDSON, MARRIED 43 YEARS

# LOW POINT
## (PART 2)

*As for me, since I am poor and needy, let the Lord keep me in his thoughts.*
*You are my helper and my savior. O my God, do not delay.*
PSALM 40:17 NLT

## SHE SAYS

I've been depressed, and I wouldn't wish it on my worst enemy. But having a spouse go through depression? It almost felt worse.

I felt so helpless. Carey asked for ideas but then wouldn't implement them. He vented and complained and made endless plans about ways he could change his circumstances, and I tried to encourage him to instead change his mind-set. I knew a different house or job wouldn't help.

He wouldn't—or couldn't—listen.

I did try to take care of myself, set healthy boundaries, and pray. At a certain point, I insisted Carey find someone other than me to talk to. He had barricaded himself from friends and others, and I had become his counselor, best friend, job coach, prayer partner, and lover. It was too much. I needed space; I needed to breathe. When he found a few trustworthy people to confide in, we both were helped.

Men, you need male friends, just like women need female friends. Satan loves to isolate Christians and keep them from the healing aspects of community. But we need other people in the body of Christ to help us be whole.

The enemy of our souls also loves to keep believers in bondage to fear, discouragement, and shame. Don't let your secret struggle destroy you. Bring it into the light, and let God heal the darkest parts of your soul. He *is* the light, and He has provided a light for your path. He will be faithful to lead you to healing waters—but you must want to get well.

For the wives of struggling husbands, I offer three loving pieces of advice—things I learned the hard way when Carey was deeply depressed.

First, remember that *you are not your husband's savior.* Listen to him, love him, and support him. Encourage him to get the help he needs—but realize that you can't fix his depression. A wise mentor told me that I was not responsible for Carey's happiness, and that helped me immensely.

Second, *take care of yourself.* Don't let yourself get so sucked into your spouse's illness that you begin to sink under the mire of depression, too. For the sake of your health and the health of your family, set appropriate boundaries and make time for the things that feed your spirit.

Third—and this may be the hardest one of all—*don't give up.* Don't let Satan talk you into the false belief that there is no hope. With Jesus, there is always hope.

The road back to a healthy mind, spirit, and body is a long, difficult road. It may involve dietary and exercise modifications, medical help, and counseling. It might take longer than you anticipated, and it will most definitely feel lonely and frustrating at times.

Nevertheless, *you can make it.* With God's help and your unceasing love for each other, you can walk through the darkest season of your life together and emerge stronger and more unified.

We pray that one day in the not too distant future, you both will experience hope, laughter, and love again.

*Jesus, the book of Isaiah says You were a man of sorrows and acquainted with grief. Thank You that You identify with us when we are struggling. When we're drowning in sorrow, give us the courage to tell others. Break the yoke of fear and shame. Lead us to wise helpers, Lord, when our bodies are broken. And thank You for never leaving us, not for a second.*

## TAKING OFF THE GLOVES
- What has been the lowest point in your marriage?
- Why was that time the worst?
- How did you make it through?
- If your lowest point is one you're currently experiencing, talk about ways to find hope.

## TIPS FROM THE PROS
*These things got us through rough times: reading scriptures; talking often throughout the day; feeding each other with good meals; drawing a warm bath, lighting candles and giving each other time alone; praying for each other; touching each other: just a shoulder squeeze and brief back rub to let the other know we were there; saying "I love you" often; always kissing each other good night.*
—JOE AND NANCY BOYD, MARRIED 13 YEARS

# SETTING THE PACE

*For God is not a God of disorder but of peace—*
*as in all the congregations of the Lord's people.*
1 CORINTHIANS 14:33

## SHE SAYS

Carey and I have had our share of problems, but he has always been good at leaving work at work. Even though he has had demanding jobs, I am grateful for his commitment to making home a place of respite. Of course, he doesn't do this perfectly, and neither do I. However, it's important to both of us that home be a place of peace and renewal, not stress.

One way I try to keep home peaceful is to be consistent about certain routines. On the days I leave the house for my part-time teaching job, I try to start the dishes and laundry and straighten our living areas before I get in the car. I also make our bed (a newer addition to the routine). That way, when we come home from work, we don't see messes waiting.

I also find it relaxing to cook at night, and Carey or my youngest son will often join me in the kitchen. I've come up with several different easy meals that are healthy and simple to make. Eating together is a ritual we don't always make time for—life and its commitments get in the way—but when we do, it grounds us and gives us a chance to have conversation about our lives in a relaxed environment.

Another favorite way to unwind and stay connected—with Carey and our boys—is walking or biking around our neighborhood or the city park. The benefit to our bodies is a bonus.

## HE SAYS

I'm pretty sure that no one has ever run a half marathon without posting about it on social media. Evidently, if you don't brag about fitness accomplishments, they don't exist. Personally, I don't have much to boast about in this area.

I've been in and out of about three different running "phases" in my life. The most dedicated one lasted for the better part of a year, and the most lackluster commitment lasted for about as long as it takes to unlace my shoes and open a bag of Doritos.

One thing I learned from my brief time as a runner is that it always benefited me to train with a friend, usually someone who was more accomplished than me (which wasn't hard to find). Having someone else set the pace pushed me forward and allowed me to get better results than if I went at it alone.

Husbands, I've also discovered that it's important for me to "set the right pace" in our home. Attitudes, whether sweet or sour, can be contagious. When I've brought my work stress home or let a bad day translate to harsh tones around the house, it's usually not long before one or more family members start emotionally running alongside me. Similarly, when I choose a pleasant, more Christlike disposition, Dena and the kids tend to get in step with that, too.

One thing I try to remember on the way home from work is to steady myself in prayer: *Lord, whatever kind of day it's been, I recognize that right now, as I walk through my front door, is the most important part of my day. Help me focus on You and be surrendered to Your Holy Spirit's guidance as I have the privilege of being a husband and a dad. I trust in You.* When I enter my home in that frame of mind and spirit, things don't always go perfectly, but they do go a lot more smoothly than if I had come in unprepared for my role.

I'm not suggesting that husbands are solely responsible for the emotional temperature in their homes. However, choosing a good attitude and yielding to God's direction *can* be an opportunity to improve our home environment as we run the race.

> *Creator God, You have given us a home, and for that we are sincerely grateful. May Your peace infuse our house as we seek to find relaxation and respite from the world's chaos.*

## TAKING OFF THE GLOVES

- Talk about the atmosphere in your home. Is it stressful, peaceful, or a mixture of both?
- Share ideas about ways to make your abode a place of harmony and not conflict.
- Is it hard for either (or both) of you to leave work at your workplace Why or why not?

## TIPS FROM THE PROS

*We were married for fifty-three years, and he still called me his bride.*
*Every day was a gift. Take each day as God's perfect gift!*
—GINNY THOMAS, WIDOW OF GORDON

# RUNNING JOKES

*A joyful heart is good medicine,*
*but a crushed spirit dries up the bones.*
PROVERBS 17:22 ESV

## SHE SAYS

Carey is a comedian—in both the best and worst sense of the word. He makes me laugh so hard I snort; this is a good quality. However, he also has favorite jokes he has repeated—ad nauseam—for two decades.

Two. Decades.

For instance, if one of us is eating a Caesar salad, this man of mine can't help himself from grinning and quipping, "This salad is so good, I could *et tu*" (as in "*Et tu*, Brute?"). See how funny that isn't?

I do appreciate a good joke, but not when it's repeated hundreds, maybe even thousands, of times.

That said, I am grateful for a mate with a sense of humor. Laughter lightens even the heaviest situations and keeps us bonded in fun ways. It has also provided us with countless priceless memories. (I love how doctors admit what the scriptures have said for centuries: laughter is good for your body. It increases blood and oxygen flow and even works your abdominal muscles. Score!)

Our dinner table is a lively place, full of puns and wordplay. I hope the boys will continue to bring laughter into their own homes when they marry and have kids. I also think they've learned that it's dangerous to go too far when you're teasing a family member. It's all good fun until someone gets hurt—so it's wise to know when to quit.

## HE SAYS

Every marriage has running jokes, special topics about which hubby and wife will forever tease each other. One of ours is driving skills—or should I say, *lack thereof?*

I have received exactly two traffic citations. One was for going too slow. No kidding. I was coming down a mountain pass in Yellowstone, California, and a CHiPs motorcycle cop pulled me over, informing me that I was driving too slow. Evidently, as I carefully crept down the mountainside, about fifteen cars had backed up behind me, and I was, in fact, breaking the law with such a "reckless manner." This does not make for a good story when my buddies are trading their tales of daredevil driving: "Oh yeah? Well, I once got a *slowing* ticket!" (*awkward silence*).

My other infraction involved my going a whopping twenty-five in a twenty-miles-per-hour school zone. Guess I was just feeling a little crazy that day. So to sum up, both of my tickets were for going *under* thirty miles per hour.

Then there's Dena.

The running joke about her is that she has *never* gotten a ticket—even though she has been pulled over *nine times*. I attribute this good fortune to a combination of Dena's sweet face, advanced verbal communication skills, and the fact that growing up, her dad was the county attorney for those particular officers. She once actually talked her way out of a speeding violation because her bladder was full: "Sir, I'm sorry, but I *reeeally* had to go!"

If I had tried to pull off that excuse, Officer Friendly probably would have cited me for drinking too much.

At least once every week or two, my sweetie and I interject into our relationship some good-natured ribbing about our driving pasts. And this only scratches the surface of the running jokes in our marriage. Joking around keeps things lighthearted in what can become a day-to-day grind. My only advice would be to do it with a wink and a smile and stay away from sore spots or anything mean-spirited.

Getting older is inevitable; growing up isn't.

Don't forget to play.

*Heavenly Father, thank You for laughter. It helps us not take ourselves too seriously and provides our family with precious memories. Let us not hurt each other with humor but instead find funny aspects of life to laugh about together.*

## TAKING OFF THE GLOVES

- When was the last time you belly laughed together? What tickled your funny bone(s)?
- Talk about an instance when one of you went too far in teasing the other one. How could you avoid those situations in the future?
- Make a laughter to-do list. Write down funny movies, comedians, YouTube channels, and books you could experience together when times get tough.

## TIPS FROM THE PROS

*The best advice I received as a young bride was never to put my husband down in front of others—not even jokingly. And don't use prayer requests as a veiled attempt to criticize your husband. I was encouraged to take my concerns to God and my husband first (and a trusted counselor if necessary). He needs me to be his biggest fan, and it has been a joy to be that for him.*

—NANCY OWENS FRANSON, MARRIED 31 YEARS

# CRAZY BUSY
## (PART 1)

*"Come to me, all you who are weary and burdened, and I will give you rest. Take my yoke upon you and learn from me, for I am gentle and humble in heart, and you will find rest for your souls. For my yoke is easy and my burden is light."*
MATTHEW 11:28–30

## HE SAYS

Exactly when did it happen? The response to the obligatory question "How are you doing?" used to be the equally generic "Fine" or even the occasional "I'm doing great; how about you?" But somewhere along the way, the common reply became, "Busy."

Trying to be a reasonably polite person, I often smile at folks and ask them how they're doing. It hit me one day just how many people blurt out the word *busy*. This little word has become the adjective of choice to describe our lives.

Why are we so busy? And for the record, I'm not referring to the "I've got a lot to do today" kind of busy. That's going to happen from time to time. I'm talking about the "my life is a blur of responsibilities and to-do lists (little of which I feel like I have time to enjoy), and I don't see any end in sight" kind of busy. This is the place where many of the people I meet live.

The thing that puzzles me is that, with very few exceptions (for example, family illness), the very busyness that we complain about is directly due to a series of choices that we made. We largely create our own chaos. Whether it's a job that keeps us on edge, too many extra activities for the kiddos, or saying yes to too much at church, each bit of stress is usually linked to a deliberate decision that we made to cram one more thing onto an already full plate.

So why do we choose a hectic life and then bemoan the fact that we feel harried and hurried all of the time?

## SHE SAYS

Why, indeed?

I, for one, spent many years trying to live up to other people's expectations. I wanted others to like me and to think I was a good person. . .instead of simply living the life God had planned for me. I became an expert plate spinner, and I looked like I was having a ball.

I wasn't.

When the plates began to crash and fall—I lost a job, friends moved away, we suffered a miscarriage—my world started crumbling. The silence was too loud, and with time on my hands, I realized I'd been running from God, from my childhood wounds, and from honest self-evaluation. . .for a long time.

*Hi, my name is Dena, and I am a people pleaser.*

When I began to experience panic attacks and depression, I decided I wanted to learn to please God. Period.

It took a long time—many months of therapy and medication—for me to climb out of that pit, but today I'm thankful I hit bottom so that I could learn to set healthy limits for myself and my family. I pray it doesn't take that for you.

Jesus promises to give us life "to the full"—but that doesn't mean He wants us to have an overstuffed schedule. He longs for us to rest in Him and His grace, to fully experience the worth that He died on the cross to secure for us. When we learn to listen to His guidance, we can confidently say yes to the things He is calling us to—and no to the rest.

Sometimes following Him means we will have a busy schedule. Often we'll feel stretched beyond our abilities and resources. However, we will have a stillness of soul that comes from knowing we're in the center of His will and not our own or someone else's.

*Lord of the Sabbath, slow us down. Help us find a pace that fits our family and our values. Thank You for the example You gave in Jesus. He often took time to be alone, to pray, to listen to Your voice.*

## TAKING OFF THE GLOVES

- Are both of you comfortable with the pace at which you live? Why or why not?
- When you say yes to something, are you striving to please God or people?
- Do you feel still in your soul even when you are busy? (Sit with that question awhile.) If not, ask God to show you why you might be cramming so many activities into your calendar.

## TIPS FROM THE PROS

*When we are going separate directions, such as when one of us goes on a trip, we write notes to each other. I'll put one in his suitcase, hide one in a pair of socks, or place one in his jacket pocket. Sometimes he sends me cards or letters in the mail. I have also found them taped to the bathroom mirror.*
—JAN RIDDLESBURGER, MARRIED 25 YEARS

# CRAZY BUSY
## (PART 2)

*"Be still, and know that I am God."*
PSALM 46:10

## HE SAYS

I believe a hamster-wheel existence falsely makes us *feel* more purposeful. We tend to define ourselves by what we can accomplish rather than by who we are in Christ. So, whether we like to admit it or not, we've become addicted to "activity," because on some level it makes us feel secure and important. However, we mustn't mistake commotion for motion. Just because we're busy doesn't mean we're moving forward.

The Dyers definitely haven't mastered it yet. There's always an ebb and flow to life, and we get just as busy as the next family from time to time. But we decided awhile back to spend a little less time going ninety-to-nothing with carpooling, overtime, and the blur of motion, and instead spend a little more time slowing down, looking into each other's eyes, and focusing on relationships—with each other and with God.

If your family gets to that boiling point I call "crazy busy," ask yourself whether the pace is worth the cost.

When we feel frantic, I believe the most productive thing we *can* do is sit down, rest in God, and let Him speak His steady, unhurried love to us.

## SHE SAYS

A life filled with regular moments for being—instead of just doing—is countercultural. It's also not easy. However, as people of faith, we're called to a different standard. Our lives should model groundedness and peace, not mindless activity.

If you long to "uncrazy" your schedule, here are a few tips:

- Review your current commitments with your spouse (and kiddos, if they are old enough). Talk about the *why* behind each commitment. Are you living life on purpose or speeding through your days without thinking about the reasons your calendar is crammed?
- For those things you've taken on out of obligation, a desire to keep up with others' expectations, an inability to say no (firmly and irrevocably), or because "no one else would do it," begin to think of

ways you can extract yourself from those responsibilities.

- Talk as a family about your core values. Make sure that every item on your schedule lines up with those values. (Some families also make a mission statement that they post in a prominent place. It keeps them accountable and serves as a daily reminder not to fill their schedules with empty activities.)
- Give yourself grace to fall and get up again. Culling a family schedule and creating more margin isn't a science; it's a process.

*Creator God, You made us with a need for rest and balance. Forgive us*
*for letting our greed and ambition get in the way of rest*
*and for modeling our lives after others instead of asking You how*
*You want us to live. May we seek to please You and not people.*

## TAKING OFF THE GLOVES
- Is your life full of motion or commotion?
- Discuss ways you and your spouse could make more time to "be" instead of "do."
- Does your life model peace (even if your schedule is quite full) or mindless activity? If it's the latter, how could you begin to make changes?

## TIPS FROM THE PROS
*One of the ways I honor my husband is by keeping the Sabbath and allowing*
*him the opportunity to rest and regroup from the busy week. He works so hard*
*during the week; it's nice for him to have a day without a million "honey dos."*
—AMY BRIGGS, MARRIED 25 YEARS

# FALLING OFF A BICYCLE

*So don't lose a minute in building on what you've been given, complementing your basic faith with good character, spiritual understanding, alert discipline, passionate patience, reverent wonder, warm friendliness, and generous love, each dimension fitting into and developing the others.*
2 PETER 1:5–6 MSG

## HE SAYS

I would never say that Dena is ditzy. . .but on a few occasions in our marriage, I wouldn't necessarily stop someone else from saying it.

I'm not commenting on her intelligence, mind you. She's much smarter than I am. However, there are times when the tiny synapses connecting her thoughts to her mouth misfire. Or maybe it's more of a backfire, like a lovable Ford truck.

My boys and I call these misfires "Dena-isms." Some of her friends have this disease, too. What she (or one of her friends) means to say: "He's got a mind like a steel trap." What they might actually say: "He's got a mind like a Mack truck."

After a couple of years of marriage, men learn to interpret their wives' special language. I understand that her brain and mouth messed up the phrase "It hit me like a Mack truck."

But I never break the flow of the conversation. I just smile, say, "Yes, dear," and then sneak off to write down what she said. One day I hope to cash in on her original colloquialisms with a bestselling book titled *A Bird in the Hand Gathers No Moss—and Other Things My Wife Says.*

I'm not exactly blaming these unique expressions on our kids, but it seems more than coincidence that Dena's condition intensified during—and after—both of her pregnancies. If I'm being an equal opportunist, I must admit that part of my brain melted when the boys came along, too. Currently they are seventeen and eleven, and I literally get their names mixed up on a daily basis.

As I get older, I think gray hair is actually gray matter oozing out of my brain. But what can I say? We love each other and she's stuck with me, like it or not. Sometimes you've just gotta "dance with the horse that brought ya."

## SHE SAYS

I love that Carey can laugh about my—yes, I'll admit it—ditziness. In fact, some of the best laughs we've shared have been over the strange (or accidentally tawdry) things I've said when I meant to say something else.

For instance, I once tried to explain that an almost-forgotten skill would most likely come back to him, and I said, "It's just like falling off a bicycle."

I'm thankful to have a spouse who can laugh at my faults instead of letting them annoy him to the point of resentment, and I consciously attempt to return the favor. (It's difficult to ignore the clothes on the end of the bed, especially when the pile begins to resemble Mount Everest, but I try. Sometimes I even put them away for him!)

For marriages to work long term, we have to choose our battles. Instead of thinking of your spouse's quirks as irritants, try to consider them as endearments. It's not automatic or second nature to us, but think back to your courtship—when your significant other's little idiosyncrasies made you smile. Back then you didn't complain to your girlfriends about his habit of sucking his teeth. You said, "He's so cute when he does that thing with his teeth!"

Familiarity changes our minds and even our hearts. The old saying is true: it can even breed contempt. That's one reason too many unions fail: the contempt overrides compassion and eventually wins out.

So the next time your spouse does something quirky, take a deep breath and smile. Say a quick prayer for patience, and thank God that you have a spouse—even one who annoys you. Remember all your quirks, and be grateful for a spouse who puts up with them. Finally, keep copious notes so that one day you can cash in on your spouse's most humorous faults.

*Lord, I am so thankful for the gift of my spouse. Forgive me when I focus on my spouse's quirks instead of being grateful for my spouse's presence in my life. Help me show patience when those quirks annoy me. And give my spouse the wisdom to treat me the same way.*

## TAKING OFF THE GLOVES
- Laugh together about some of the ditzy things you've done. Take turns reliving funny moments through a lens of humor and grace.
- Think about ways to help each other remember important tasks. Research apps or other free online tools. Take advantage of

technology to simplify your life!

- Discuss times when a partner's carelessness or forgetfulness affected you deeply. Share your emotions without resorting to name calling or accusations. Begin sentences with "I felt. . ." instead of "You made me. . . ." Take time to forgive each other and pray together.

## TIPS FROM THE PROS
*I spend casual time hanging out with my husband so I never forget how much I like him, even when we disagree!*
—REBECCA SIREVAAG, MARRIED 15 YEARS

# MEN ARE A MYSTERY

*God created human beings; he created them godlike, reflecting God's nature.*
*He created them male and female. . . . God looked over everything*
*he had made; it was so good, so very good!*
GENESIS 1:27, 31 MSG

## HE SAYS

We have just two sons, but when my wife introduces herself, she says that she has three boys. As it turns out, I'm the third one. I'm not sure if she's subtly implying that I'm immature (if so, I couldn't really argue with her). More likely, though, she's referring to the perpetual "guy-ness" that exists in our home. Poor Dena loves her three boys, for sure; but I know there's a part of her that longs to have a little girl who would, you know, act like a human child. Dena is a sweet, fragrant flower planted among a colony of boll weevils, which produce a completely different fragrance.

According to my nonscientific study, once our family gets home from an outing, it takes approximately eighteen seconds for the conversation to descend into some form of bathroom humor or coarse joking, followed by a chorus of bodily functions that defy description in their potency. Technological advances notwithstanding, I sometimes wonder how far men have *really* come. The TV has pretty much become the fire around which we sit, grunt, and pick our fur.

Sometimes I try to inject civility into our "manners lite" atmosphere. Once, when we were all four in the car, our youngest decided to rehearse his new trick: burping on demand. Wanting to reinforce good manners *and* get hubby brownie points at the same time, I informed him, "There's a lady in the car."

"Who is it?" he burped, sincerely confused as to whom I was talking about. *Sigh.* Guess we still have a ways to go.

## SHE SAYS

When I was growing up, I imagined myself the mother to both a boy and a girl. The girl and I would have tea parties, play dress-up, and visit the spa together. We'd shop for clothes and home furnishings, cook, and talk about the deep things of life, while looking put-together and stylish.

And then God gave me boys.

Don't get me wrong: I adore my two sons and my husband. I just don't always understand them.

Over the years, living with the male of the species has led me to questions I have no answer for, such as:

- Who would play endless video games about aliens and zombies when they could enjoy watching—and crying through—a realistic portrayal of human emotion and redemption like *Hope Floats*?
- How can Jordan, Jackson, and Carey memorize the release dates for the bajillion Marvel, X-Men, and Star Wars movies but never *ever* remember my request to pick up after themselves?
- Why are poop jokes so hilarious? I just. Don't. Get. It.

These are tough questions, I know. I'm probably going to have to wait until heaven to find out the answers.

I just hope I don't have to wait that long for a granddaughter.

*Lord, You created both the sexes and called both male and female "very good." Help us keep that in mind when we are overwhelmed with confusion and irritation at the ways we are different from each other. Also, Father, help us see each other through Your eyes rather than through our frail human ones.*

## TAKING OFF THE GLOVES

- Men will always be somewhat of a mystery to women, and vice versa. Talk about the things you're mystified by.
- Ask your spouse, "Is there something I do as a man/woman that drives you up the wall?" Be gentle and gracious with your responses.
- Encourage your partner to have friendships with other men (husbands) and women (wives) and get together with those friends regularly.

### TIPS FROM THE PROS

*As you age, marriage seems to get easier and more comfortable. I know what he thinks and how he feels about certain things and vice versa. But even with all the familiarity there are still surprises almost daily.*
—LYNDA SPURLOCK, MARRIED 22 YEARS

# HOW TO KNOW SHE'S REALLY MAD

*Sneering at others is a spark that sets a city on fire;*
*using good sense can put out the flames of anger.*
PROVERBS 29:8 CEV

## HE SAYS

A *tell* in poker is a slight change in behavior that gives away that player's assessment of his or her hand. A tell in marriage is a change in behavior that lets a husband know that he is moments away from his own demise.

Twenty years have given me plenty of time to learn to read even the most nuanced glance from Dena. We can literally pick up in the middle of a conversation we never verbally started, because I already know what she's thinking.

Her ace in the hole is a catalog of facial expressions I can translate with laser accuracy. They warn me when I am venturing into unsafe territory. Although your spouse's signals may differ, here is a decoding of my sweet bride's "special language":

- *A slight pursing of the lips.* Dena doesn't even realize that she's getting mildly annoyed at this point—but I do.

- *A slow, almost inaudible sigh through her mouth.* This is my wife's way of letting me know she is starting to get upset. It's a courtesy gesture. She's firing shots over my bow, giving me a friendly warning to choose another route.

- *Mouth closed, running her tongue underneath her top lip as she exhales through her nose.* She's just about reached her version of author Malcolm Gladwell's tipping point ("the moment of critical mass, the threshold, the boiling point"). If I'm in my right mind, I will quickly stop whatever I'm doing or saying.

- *A sudden dead stare into my eyes.* Things just got real. I'm not sure why, but this gaze causes my internal organs to shift to the left about three inches. My stomach becomes weightless, and I mentally start scribbling out a good-bye note to the kids.

- *In addition to the aforementioned stare, a quick flaring of the nostrils.* "Danger, Will Robinson!" Immediately run out of the house. In mere seconds, your neighborhood will be razed by Superman-like heat vision.

My wife is as sweet as they come, but I'm thankful that she has tells—so I know when to fold.

## SHE SAYS

Carey is like the main character in the song "The Gambler." He knows when to hold 'em, when to fold 'em, when to walk away, and when to run.

As it says in *The Husband's Bible*, "A man who knows how to read his wife lives a long life" (Hesitations 5:11).

> *God, thank You for body language. It gives us ways to read our*
> *spouse's emotions when they—or we—don't know what is wrong.*
> *Help us learn to translate each other's facial expressions and*
> *gestures so that we can better communicate with each other.*

## TAKING OFF THE GLOVES

- Talk about the ways—body language, expressions, noises—each of you communicates when the other is irritating you.
- Take some time to apologize and forgive each other for the ways you've clashed recently.
- Ask your spouse, "Is there something I could stop doing that would make our marriage better for you?" and "Is there something I could start doing that would make our union stronger?" Then follow through.

### TIPS FROM THE PROS

*A little laughter can diffuse or put into perspective so many situations.*
*Then talking in a nondefensive fashion can follow. Tell each*
*other you love each other a lot—and mean it.*
—DEBBIE DACUS, MARRIED 28 YEARS

# WHEN A TOASTER
# MARRIES A CROCK-POT

*If anyone loudly blesses their neighbor early
in the morning, it will be taken as a curse.*
PROVERBS 27:14

## HE SAYS

*Shhh. As we carefully approach the roofed habitation, let us now observe
the early morning rituals of the North American* Homo sapiens. *You'll notice
that this particular diurnal male's low rousing threshold causes him to function
at a relatively high level at first dawn's light. However, his mate suffers from
hypersomnia, or excessive sleeping, to the extent that her circadian rhythms can
only be interrupted by the internal application of* Coffea canephora, *also known
as the common coffee bean. Until said bean extract is liquefied and consumed, the
female is characterized by melancholy moods and harsh tones.*

I wake up like a toaster, sometimes literally jumping out of bed. I
understand this is annoying to about half the population. As a matter of
fact, some folks would probably haul off and slap me if they saw me cheerily
bounding out of my slumber. I think the Lord may have had people like me
in mind when He inspired Proverbs 27:14, because boy, can I loudly bless!

Dena wakes up more like a Crock-Pot set on low. . .no, make that *warm*.
On some Saturdays, it's more of a completely unplugged Crock-Pot, at least
until noon. She considers her alarm not as a call to arms, but more as a
suggestion to roll over and go back to sleep. Her alarm sounds exactly like
mine, but we have completely different reactions.

In fact, I recently had Dena's alarm analyzed by Princeton University's
sleep research lab. They ran the sound of her alarm through a universal
translator. In English, it's saying: "Hey friend, no big deal, but it's 7:30 a.m.,
which I know is crazy early. So, I'll tell you what: if you wanna just tap me on
the head where it says 'snooze,' I'll remind you in about ten minutes how late
you're gonna be for work. And for heaven's sake, go back to sleep!"

## SHE SAYS

Sleep and energy differences were one of the main things that caused
us conflict in the early years of our marriage. Carey's father believes that
staying in bed past seven thirty will give him bedsores. On the other hand,

my mother was a champion sleeper. I think she might actually have a listing in the *Guinness Book of World Records* for "Person Staying in Bed the Longest without Being Sick." She has even trained Dad to bring her coffee in bed every morning so she can wake up slowly while "savoring the flavor" (as she calls it).

To Carey, my sleeping in on Saturdays smacked of laziness and selfishness. I felt entitled to sleep in because I had worked hard all week, and with my physical issues, I need more sleep than he does.

Cue the awful arguments on weekends. I felt attacked and he felt disrespected. Looking back, we might have avoided most of the conflict by honestly talking about our respective family upbringings.

Because we were on the road while planning the wedding, we didn't make time for premarital counseling (we were so in love—what could go wrong?). Yikes. It's something we regret. With the experience of years and hard-earned wisdom, we highly recommend godly counseling before and during marriage, especially when big conflicts threaten to derail your home's harmony.

Over time we came to an arrangement that suits both of us: I don't sleep past ten on Saturdays, so I don't miss the whole morning. I still get rest, but I'm not robbing us of tons of together time. Carey tries to understand my need for extra sleep, and he even brings me coffee in bed sometimes.

That, ladies and gentlemen, is what's called progress.

*Lord, thank You for the ways You made us. Forgive us when we lose patience*
*with each other over the differences in our energy levels, personalities,*
*or expectations. Help us see each other through the lens of grace and gratitude.*

## TAKING OFF THE GLOVES

- What are some differences causing conflict in your marriage?
- How have you resolved them, or are you still working on resolving them?
- What regrets do you have from your engagement or newlywed years? Take turns discussing them together—with honesty, humility, and compassion.

## TIPS FROM THE PROS

*Have grace for each other. We're in this together till the end.*
*We can make it pleasant, or we can make it miserable. I choose pleasant.*
—JANET FLIPPIN, MARRIED 33 YEARS

# THE WEDDING SINGER (PART 1)

*This is my beloved, this is my friend.*
Song of Songs 5:16

## SHE SAYS

I was a bridesmaid eight—count 'em, eight!—times before I was ever a bride. At each wedding, I gained ideas for my own future ceremony, wonderful memories from the weekend of activities, and an expensive dress that I never wore again.

That said, I truly enjoyed most of my bridesmaid duties. I loved standing with the bride and watching her face, and the groom's, when they saw each other for the first time. I treasured lots of girl time with my closest friends before they became wedded to their mates. And I truly appreciated being asked to witness and participate in such happy occasions.

No wedding was perfect, though. In one ceremony—where I served as maid of honor—the flower girl sneezed and a big ball of snot dangled from her nose. I leaned over and handed her a tissue, which I had cleverly concealed in my bouquet. She wiped her nose and hands—and handed it back. Shortly after that lovely moment, the photographer almost fell out of the balcony.

With all my experience, I knew exactly what I wanted to happen at my wedding—and what I didn't want. My rules: No children in the ceremony (in one unforgettable wedding, a child had blurted out, "When's the baby due?" in the middle of the vows, because she thought getting married meant having an infant). No ugly or expensive dresses for my attendants (I found a place that rented the frocks to my friends). No long, embarrassing kiss at the altar.

Our wedding weekend had a few glitches—but nothing serious. My mom turned over the unity candle, but it wasn't lit. And the minister said, "Do you, Dena, take Carey to be your lawfully wedded wife?" Still, it was everything I could have hoped for, and more.

Reception with a string quartet and candles (a church fellowship hall had never looked so beautiful—thanks, Mom!)? Check. Rehearsal dinner at the ranch, complete with chuck wagon cookout and perfect weather? Check. Time with friends and family, celebrating the love God had given Carey and me? Check.

## HE SAYS

By my best guess, I've sung at forty or fifty weddings. Most of the time, I knew the couple in some capacity, and other times, believe it or not, I've just been a "hired gun"—called on by strangers to sing some love songs because evidently none of their friends or family members knew "Love Me Tender."

My compensation for being a wedding crooner has ranged from cash to key chains to calligraphy-engraved pocket knives (so I can cut off zip ties with elegance). As a matter of fact, where I grew up in Tennessee, I think the term *shotgun wedding* refers to the fact that a firearm is an acceptable groomsmen gift.

Once, as a broke college student, I got paid reeeally well by a doctor who was footing the bill for his daughter's big event. Expensive? I didn't know that many bride's attendants could fit on one church stage. The wedding cake had its own valet parking. I can't relate. We were so poor, we just got married for the rice. . .but seriously.

I have no objections to expensive weddings for those who can actually afford them. It's a special day on which we place a lot of value. However, I'm sometimes perplexed at how much is spent on the wedding in relation to how little has been spent preparing for the marriage.

Seeking wisdom from someone with a successful marriage is wise (and free!). The sweet elderly couple who holds hands and sits on the same row in your church every Sunday morning is still together for a reason, and chances are they have more relationship knowledge in their heads and hearts than a Kindle full of books.

So don't just put all of your time, effort, and expenses into *the* day. Prepare for the long haul, and seek help from those who have traveled it before.

*Father, thank You for the love we've been given. Help us put as much effort, time, and expense into our day-to-day union as we did into our marriage ceremony.*

## TAKING OFF THE GLOVES

- How expensive was your wedding? What is the most expensive one you've ever attended?
- How did you prepare for marriage? How are you still investing in your union?
- Talk about ways you could continue to invest in your relationship

(examples: yearly or quarterly retreats, marriage conferences, regular date nights/days).

## TIPS FROM THE PROS

*Be willing to work on things that can better build your marriage. Surround yourself with good people and get involved in your church home.*
—Kayla Freeman, married 10 years

# NOTES

# NOTES

# PART 5

# STILL STANDING

# THE WEDDING SINGER (PART 2)

*His mouth is sweetness itself; he is altogether lovely.*
*This is my beloved, this is my friend, daughters of Jerusalem.*
SONG OF SONGS 5:16

## HE SAYS

Whereas I've lent my singing voice to weddings-a-plenty, it wasn't until recently that I was asked to actually officiate my first wedding. I knew what the minister's role was, but when it came to hitting my mark up front, next to the couple (starting with "We are gathered here today. . ."), it proved to be a completely different experience. The day was deeply meaningful in a whole new way.

The groom had been a student in my youth ministry several years back, and when I got the call, I was honored to be considered for such an important task. For my first time in the driver's seat, my annoying attention to detail was in full bloom: all of my notes for the ceremony typed out and pasted into a nondescript black journal, with an extra copy of said notes tucked into my wife's purse. I wore a simple black suit and tie and did a fully voice-projected run-through of the ceremony on my own (even rehearsing my two funny lines and pausing where the laughter would go). I put a bow on my preparation by praying Beth Moore's famous "Lord, show up or I'm toast." I was good to go.

I think today's weddings display some of the best revisions of time-honored traditions. When I got married in the mid-1990s, almost every ceremony included full tuxedos and fluffy dresses. Weddings were a formal affair, after all. I'm refreshed by the slightly-more-laid-back-but-still-elegant vibe of many weddings today. Blake, the groom whose ceremony I led, sported Air Jordan sneakers with his casual suit. He encouraged me to wear my orange Converse kicks with my suit, but I chickened out.

Perhaps my favorite part was the replacement of the traditional unity candle with a unity sand ceremony. The bride and groom each pour sand into a third empty vessel. Just as the mixed sand is nigh impossible to separate, so the couple is fused together by God's love in holy matrimony.

There was something extraspecial about having the best seat in the house and leading Blake and Kristen in their vows. I felt privileged, much like being present at a child's birth, to be up close and personal at the genesis of a married life. As they teared up reciting their vows, there's a slight chance that I may have dabbed the corner of my eye as well.

## SHE SAYS

Like Carey, I've sung at more than a few ceremonies. I always feel honored to be part of such a momentous occasion—and I adored seeing Carey lead a young couple in their vows.

I could tell he was nervous; after all, singing in a wedding is nerve-wracking, because you want to do your best and not mess up the ceremony. But officiating? That's another level of pressure altogether.

But he did a great job, just as I knew he would. I loved the humor he injected, which lightened the tension and helped everyone feel comfortable. Carey has a gift for making people feel at ease and for lightening moods. It's a gift he's used in our marriage many times.

I'm a very serious person and I can be my own worst enemy. Carey helps me laugh in the midst of chaos (and even brings the chaos sometimes!) and laugh at myself. I have often given thanks to God for his ability to know the right words to say when I'm stressed. His positive approach to life has balanced out my more cautious, pessimistic (I call it "realistic") personality.

Once again God knew what He was doing when He matched us up. I felt the same way when I attended Blake and Kristen's wedding. We were blessed to be a part of their big day.

*God, thank You for creating marriage so that a man and wife can become one flesh. We praise You for the way You work; we adore You for bringing beauty from ashes. You are a glorious God!*

## TAKING OFF THE GLOVES

- Do you have a favorite wedding tradition? What is it, and why is it your favorite?
- What's your favorite memory from your own wedding ceremony? Why?
- Read the story of Jesus' first recorded miracle at the wedding at Cana. Why do you think He chose to reveal His miracle-working power there?

## TIPS FROM THE PROS

*We give and give in a way we think love should be expressed—*
*only to find we are not appreciated. Learn what makes*
*your spouse feel valued, and do those things.*
—BILL VRIESEMA, MARRIED 34 YEARS

# LOST WEDDING RINGS

*"For the Son of Man came to seek and to save the lost."*
LUKE 19:10

## HE SAYS

The list of dumb things I've done since being married is longer than the list of televangelists with bad wigs. However, some of my marital misdeeds rise to hall of fame status.

Losing my wedding ring wasn't really that stupid. Accidents happen. Of course, even with my limited understanding of Spanish, swimming in a body of water called the Frio River should have tipped me off that colder-than-normal water *might* make my fingers shrink—enough to let my gold band slip off and fall to the silty bottom. . .where it sits today. I didn't realize it until the next morning. The absence almost startled me awake: "My ring!" It's the one thing I'd had on since our wedding day.

The dumb part starts with the weeks. . .okay, months. . .okay, *years*, I let pass by without replacing the ring. (This wasn't exactly a warm, fuzzy topic around our house.)

For a while, I was in denial about never getting back my original ring. I fantasized about a dramatic story of biblical proportions: I return to the river, catch a catfish, and—lo and behold—what's in its mouth? I thought such a miracle would at least make it into the human-interest segment at the end of the local newscast, if not propel me to a national platform. "Yes, Matt, I was just as surprised as anyone, and that's no fish tale!" (Insert Matt Lauer fake-laughing at my pun.)

But alas, no. There was no dramatic story, no lost-and-found call from the bait shop. Just my prized possession at the bottom of a river next to bottle tops and tangled fishing line.

After I gave up hope of getting back my original ring, I just didn't get around to replacing it. If that sounds cold, unromantic, and kind of idiotic, then you've assessed correctly. *Two years* passed, and I finally got another wedding band. Luckily, I got to keep the same wife, although she was slightly perturbed.

## SHE SAYS

Lest you think too badly about Carey, I have a story of my own. A few years into our marriage, when Carey was a youth minister and I was pregnant with our oldest son, my fingers began to swell. During one particular weekend, I had accompanied Carey to a youth conference at a large hotel. At one point during the conference, I took off my wedding band and engagement ring and put them in my purse.

Later I realized that they had either fallen out or been taken by someone. I never found them.

However, instead of getting mad at me, Carey was sympathetic and understanding (two traits, among others, that he has had to practice regularly during our union because of my lack of attention to detail).

On our next wedding anniversary, after a splendid meal, we ended up at a beautiful botanical garden in Fort Worth, where my forever-beau got down on one knee and presented me with a replacement ring set. This one had a bigger stone in it, too.

He's a jewel.

Through lost rings and lost tempers, I've been grateful for something Carey has told me more than once when we've suffered disappointment or distress: "Things are just things. Our relationship is what's important."

The same is true about our relationship to God. No matter what we go through or what we lose, He is the one constant. He never changes, and He never loses His grip on us.

*Merciful Jesus, in the Gospels You shared stories of lost coins, lost sheep, and lost souls. Good Shepherd, You gave Yourself to find the lost. We are forever grateful for Your extravagant grace. Help us never lose sight of You as we journey together through married life.*

## TAKING OFF THE GLOVES

- Talk about something valuable or sentimental one of you has misplaced. How did it make you feel?
- Have you lost intangibles in your relationship—joy, humor, intimacy? How does that make you feel?
- Think and pray together about ways you could recapture some of the above. Ask a mentor couple or counselor to help you if you get stuck or need ideas and/or prayer.

## TIPS FROM THE PROS

*Everyone experiences trouble and crises, but those are pivotal points in a marriage, where you can honor the vows you spoke—or listen to what the world has to say.*
—CHER THOMPSON, MARRIED 35 YEARS

# SEX—NOW AND THEN

*May your fountain be blessed,*
*and may you rejoice in the wife of your youth.*
PROVERBS 5:18

## HE SAYS

Newlyweds: once every two hours.
After twenty-five years: two hours after the medicine kicks in.

Newlyweds: too aroused to sleep.
Twenty-five years: too asleep to rouse.

Newlyweds: "I can't get enough of you."
Twenty-five years: "Isn't that enough? Whew!"

Honeymoon: "You drive me crazy!"
Twenty-five years: "You're driving me crazy!"

Writing about sex is exactly as awkward as it sounds. And yet we'd be remiss to barely touch on the topic that's kept men hoping and women nope-ing since the Garden of Eden.

Sex is kind of like golf. One day it's amazing and you can do no wrong as you score your best. Then another time it's cumbersome, you end up tired and angry, and at least one of you thinks, *I should've stayed back and had a club sandwich.*

But once again I feel like God in His infinite wisdom made sex hit-or-miss and, frankly, kind of a weird act for a specific purpose. I think there's a reason that men are like frying pans and women are more like slow cookers. It's one more opportunity for us to be patient, go against our natural bent, and be self*less.*

Like most husbands, I'm more, shall we say, easily excited, while Dena likes to be wooed and cherished leading up to the act. Think about it. For sexual intimacy to be mutually enjoyable, it almost always takes two people going against their natural tendencies and giving to the other. I think that's the difference between plain old intercourse and physical intimacy. You're not simply getting something; you're giving of yourself to bond with the one that God has given you.

So, how does this translate to everyday life? Men, sometimes we need to learn to put it in first gear, decelerate, and opt for the Indy 500 over the drag race. That will often mean whispering something sweet in her ear on your way out the door in the morning, texting her that you're thinking about her during the day, and putting the kids to bed by yourself that night—in anticipation of what's to come. Conversely, wives, knowing that men love spontaneity and variety, surprise him from time to time with something spur of the moment, and be open to a sprint instead of a marathon.

## SHE SAYS

Contrary to Carey's funny opening scenarios, our sexual intimacy—and our enjoyment of it—has only increased as the years have gone by.

Why? I believe it's because we've both been willing to learn about the other, stay interesting and interested in each other, and make that part of our lives a priority. We've also found resources (a favorite is Bill and Pam Farrel's book, *Red-Hot Monogamy*) that have helped us in the bedroom.

Our culture says it's more fun to "hook up" casually and have sex outside of a marriage covenant. God's so-much-better plan is for a couple to grow together in every way: spiritual, emotional, physical. Sex, at its best, is an opportunity to give of yourself and celebrate your mate. And when you give, you receive—far more than you could imagine.

What could be more exciting than that?

*We thank You, Father, for the gift of sexual intimacy. Help us treasure our sexual relationship and give it the priority it deserves. Let us not take each other for granted or be selfish. Forgive us when we put our needs and desires above our spouse's. Draw us closer to You and to each other.*

## TAKING OFF THE GLOVES

- Do you relate to Carey's funny opening to this piece?
- How would you rate your sexual relationship on a scale of one to ten?
- What could improve your score? Talk honestly and openly about the issues you face and how each of you could unselfishly move toward resolution of any problems. (Note: If one or both of you has been abused, we know this can be a very tough subject to navigate. We

are so sorry you've been through such pain, and we pray that God will heal and restore what has been wounded and lost. We highly recommend professional Christian counseling to deal with the many repercussions of abuse.)

## TIPS FROM THE PROS

*My husband cherishes me every day in the way he treats me. Whenever I answer the phone, he always says, "Hello, Beautiful!" It gets me every time. How we speak to each other and the way we say things matter.*
—AMY BRIGGS, MARRIED 25 YEARS

# HITTING THE MATTRESS

*So we do not lose heart. Though our outer self is wasting away,*
*our inner self is being renewed day by day.*
2 CORINTHIANS 4:16 ESV

## HE SAYS

Some time ago I stopped referring to the two of us as "getting older" and started saying that we were "more seasoned," which seems less severe, although it makes us sound like entrees. One of the times our seasoning shows up is in our bedtime routine. (It's not what you think.)

Once you hit age forty, it takes a combination of soothing teas, pills, and contraptions to actually achieve sleep. When we first started having trouble sleeping, we blamed it on our mattress. (It's not that humbling to admit that your *mattress* is getting more seasoned.)

We'd heard a lot about Tempur-Pedic mattresses. However, Tempur-Pedic is evidently the Latin term for "sell your car," which is what we would have to do to afford one. People sleep better on them because they are rich. If I had four grand to drop on a mattress, I could probably sleep easy on a burlap sack full of grass clippings.

After a couple of doctor visits, we finally admitted that our respective sleeping problems were due to our bodies breaking down a bit. I was grinding my teeth in my sleep, which means I'm even hyper while at rest. This was easily solved with a hard plastic mouth guard that clips onto my front teeth to prevent me from biting down. It also makes me speak with an inebriated southern drawl.

Dena wasn't achieving REM sleep, which at first I thought had something to do with a rock band. Instead, it meant she wasn't sleeping deeply enough. Her issue actually attained the status of a "disorder," so it cost a lot more to fix than a mere "problem." It was resolved with a CPAP machine, basically a diving tank plugged into the wall. Once it's turned on, she achieves a blissful sleep by putting on a fighter-pilot mask and breathing through a hose.

So, there we were at bedtime: me in my slobbery mouth guard and Dena hooked up to her breathing mask. Ahh, let the evening romance ensue. It's like Forrest Gump and Darth Vader trying to get cozy every night.

## SHE SAYS

Romantic, right? Getting older is humbling, if not downright ridiculous. Things are sagging, sprouting, and spreading out all over. Some days, it's like a Broadway musical-meets-horror-film around here.

However, aging isn't all bad. Yes, it takes more equipment to get around these days, but we've lost some baggage over the years, too.

It's true that over the last two decades, I've seen Carey in some pretty embarrassing getups—and he's seen me in all variations of fat, thin, and in between. But mostly I've seen him mature into a godly leader who isn't afraid of what people think and who demonstrates Christ's love by serving unselfishly. By the grace of God, he's laid aside insecurities that used to trip him up and grabbed onto the unwavering love of Jesus. It's a beautiful thing to behold.

For my part, I've traded in perfectionist tendencies that once held me captive and traded Satan's lies about my worth for my heavenly Father's unconditional love. I know that Carey, Jordan, and Jackson have benefited from the work I've done unlearning old patterns, setting healthy boundaries, and retraining my mind to focus on the lovely, holy things of God rather than on the multitude of anxieties that used to plague me.

I wouldn't trade our experiences (even the difficult ones) for anything, because they've made us who we are, right now.

*Heavenly Father, thank You for Your presence with us as we get older. Help us see the humor in our changing bodies, and thank You that in Christ we never really die. Give us courage to face the changes that aging brings and grace to accept each other as we are.*

## TAKING OFF THE GLOVES

- How has getting older changed your relationship? If it hasn't yet, how do you see it affecting you?
- Has your bedtime routine gotten stale or even downright ridiculous? Discuss ways to up the romance factor a bit.
- Talk about senior adults you both admire. What makes them inspirational?

## TIPS FROM THE PROS

*Remember your first love. Review the old photos,*
*relive those early days. Talk about your memories.*
—SANDRA AND DENNIS KING, MARRIED 47 YEARS

# WHEN LIFE'S A PAIN

*"Even to your old age and gray hairs I am he, I am he who will sustain you.*
*I have made you and I will carry you; I will sustain you and I will rescue you."*
Isaiah 46:4

## HE SAYS

A heads-up to all the young whippersnappers out there: as soon as you hit forty, you need to clear off a space on your kitchen counter for pills. I'm not talking about a small, toaster-sized area. You may eventually have to build on an extra room to house your prescription bottles.

I'm convinced that you can tell a person's age by how many pills he or she takes. It's like counting the rings on a redwood tree. When my parents come to visit, they bring a rolling suitcase just for pills. By the time age fifty gets here, Dena and I will have made the transition from "prayer and meditation" to "prayer and medication."

The other day I actually hurt my neck throwing back my head to swallow a pill. Good thing it was for pain!

What are all these meds for? Most of the pills make you stop doing things. Some actually help you start doing things. If you meet anyone over forty who tells you they don't take any pills, they're lying—or they just forgot to take their medication.

In all seriousness, aging is an aspect of life God never meant for us to fear. We should embrace it as part of how He made us. You are exactly the age He wants you to be right now. Every mass media outlet screams at us to run from old age like the plague. However, there are unique joys at every stage of life. And even as our bodies begin to break down a bit, God is ever with us—pills and all.

## SHE SAYS

I've heard the encouraging phrases "Age is just a number" and "You're only as old as you feel" countless times, and while they may be true, I don't discount the grief we feel as we get older. Every year we age brings with it challenges—physical, mental, emotional, financial, and relational—that we might not anticipate. Sometimes the changes we're forced to accept feel momentous, and some are simply devastating.

I've met a lot of cranky older folks, and while I can understand why they may feel that way (loss of control, fear of being left behind, anger at being sidelined), I *really* don't want to be one of them.

Friends, let's not live as if we are without hope. Let's not swallow the devil's lies (such as younger is better and outward beauty is all that matters).

Paul writes that "though outwardly we are wasting away, yet inwardly we are being renewed day by day" (2 Corinthians 4:16). As believers in Jesus, if we continue to surrender daily to His plans and seek after His will, we become gentler, kinder, and more loving. Scripture teaches that when we see Him in heaven, we will be like Him and we'll see Him as He is (1 John 3:2).

Now that's something to look forward to!

*Abba Father, our bodies are changing daily. Thank You for Your presence and perspective as we face getting older, together. Help us keep a sense of humor about the ups and downs of this earthly life. We praise You for the gift of heaven and eagerly await meeting You face-to-face one day.*

## TAKING OFF THE GLOVES

- What most concerns you about getting older? Why?
- How have your parents aged? What kinds of things can you learn from them (or vow to do differently)?
- Look up routines from clean comedians like Tim Hawkins, Brian Regan, and Anita Renfroe on getting older. Watch them together and laugh about some of the absurdities of life.

## TIPS FROM THE PROS

*We make each other a priority. What this looks like has changed over time. As newlyweds, we enjoyed simple things like walks and talks. With young kids, we got them to bed on time and had date nights at home. With crazy-busy school-aged kids, we banished them (all ages) by 9:00 p.m. and enjoyed television, talking, and time together before calling it a night. Now we have only two kids at home. We go on regular date nights and give each other time to pursue friends and interests away from home. Sitting together in the evening after the kids' bedtime is part of our regular routine.*
—SHARON EDWARDS, MARRIED 25 YEARS

# FOR RICHER, FOR POORER

*"I am the vine; you are the branches. Whoever abides in me and I in him,*
*he it is that bears much fruit, for apart from me you can do nothing."*
JOHN 15:5 ESV

## HE SAYS

". . .for richer, for poorer." I think back to when we faced each other and said those words on our magic day. Little did we know the lean times that lay ahead. Oh, we knew we would have financially sparse times. I mean, we were *already* broke when we uttered that phrase.

With both of us working in the fluctuating field of the arts, we've come to expect an ebb and flow to our income. It's the emotionally and spiritually poor times that have been the most trying.

Brace yourself: sometimes you don't feel like being married.

It's true. When we were newlyweds, I wouldn't have believed that. But a decade and a half later, I was dissatisfied with where I was in life. My job, our finances, my usual life-of-the-party persona, even my spiritual life—everything had seemed to dry up. My very soul felt poor.

I began to project the way I felt onto Dena. She was there, so it was convenient. Although I didn't realize it at the time, I started to shift the blame for my condition onto her. In anger one day, referring to where I was in life, I yelled, "Well, I've got to get out of here, whether you're coming or not!"

Wow. I had never said anything close to that before. I didn't even know I felt that way until those words escaped my mouth. I hadn't used the big *D* word, but the implication was there. It was a big reality check on how far down I'd slid. It took awhile, but I finally started getting some help. Dena (bless her sweet, long-suffering heart) stayed with me all the way.

It became a defining moment for me, because in my pride I had always thought those types of hardships were for *other* couples.

God showed me that remaining in a right relationship with Him and with my bride doesn't just passively happen. It takes a deliberate, even stubborn kind of love to stay together "for richer, for poorer."

## SHE SAYS

I remember that day well. How could I forget? I think my response to Carey was something along the lines of "Well, if you need to leave, then do it!"

Sometimes marriage isn't fun. At times it's downright difficult. And at other times it's a long, slow slog through the muck. (Like a Spartan race, only less muddy.)

"Loving each other with the endurance only God can give" isn't part of the typical wedding vows, but maybe it should be. In a union of two imperfect people, one or both of you will sometimes feel like running from your responsibilities. At certain moments, one or both of you may be tempted to emotionally or physically cheat on your spouse.

Those forks in the road are important. If you turn to God and ask for His strength to stay together, He promises to give you the forbearance you need to keep your wedding vows.

Unless one of you has abandoned the other through abuse, betrayal, or neglect, divorce is never ideal. (Even in those circumstances, God can bring healing and reconciliation if the offending party chooses to change their behavior and seek forgiveness.)

Please hear us: divorce is *not* an unforgivable sin, and in some cases it may be the best path to take. Only God knows what goes on in marriages, and we know that remaining married is sometimes downright dangerous. However, divorce *is* a tearing of the fabric God weaves when He joins two people in holy matrimony.

We've heard it said that for a marriage to last, it takes two people who are both 100 percent committed to the marriage. Carey and I believe it takes three people: a man, a wife, and Jesus. Without Him, we don't have the fortitude to make the right choices again and again.

Without Him, we won't make it.

*We need You, Jesus. . .desperately. Hold us together in the times*
*we feel like we can't hold on. Thank You for never letting go of us.*

## TAKING OFF THE GLOVES

- Did either of you come into marriage from a divorced family?
- If so, how did that affect you? If not, what did you learn about marriage (good or bad) from parents who stayed married?
- Decide together never to utter the *D* word, even as a joke. This one piece of advice has greatly helped us over the years.

## TIPS FROM THE PROS

*My wife listens, and when the time is right, she always seems to help me see the situation from a better, more eternal perspective.*
—BRYAN BUFKIN, MARRIED 8 YEARS

# LET IT GO

*The world doesn't fight fair. But we don't live or fight our battles that way—*
*never have and never will. . . . We use our powerful God-tools for smashing*
*warped philosophies, tearing down barriers erected against the truth of God,*
*fitting every loose thought and emotion and impulse into the structure of life*
*shaped by Christ. Our tools are ready at hand for clearing the ground of*
*every obstruction and building lives of obedience into maturity.*

2 CORINTHIANS 10:3–6 MSG

## HE SAYS

Don't sweat the small stuff.

Take it easy.

Let it go.

No, I'm not listing a combination of inspiring posters and Disney song titles. The above clichés, trite as they may be, actually have merit in our day-to-day lives as married couples.

At times Dena and I have had knock-down, drag-out fights, but after a while, we're so emotionally worn out from arguing, we can't even remember what started the whole thing. One moment a dirty undershirt is left on the floor, and in thirty minutes we're rehashing the Great Toilet Seat Incident of '97.

I've learned the hard way that being right at all costs isn't worth bruising my relationship with Dena. Who really cares who left the refrigerator open? I mean, we wouldn't argue about such trivial things with a stranger on the street, yet somehow within the confines of marriage, we feel like those petty grievances are worth a bout of verbal sparring.

I can spend way too much time expressively flailing around and trying to emotionally control a moment ("I'll prove her wrong! The Beatles *were* better than the Stones!") instead of taking a few deep breaths and asking myself one simple question: Is all of this intensity really worth it?

Have you noticed that, by and large, elderly couples don't argue much? Oh, I'm sure they have their moments of griping like anyone else, but the older couples I've spent time with seem to have quieted any high-pitched dissonance down to a nice, harmonious hum.

I believe many of them have discovered what I'm still trying to learn: as husband and wife, we have limited earthly resources and only so much time together. Let's not spend it majoring on the minors. Let's use our time talking about real joys and struggles, not petty issues we'll have forgotten about before the ink is dry on the conversation.

PS: But seriously, the Beatles really *were* better than the Rolling Stones.

## SHE SAYS

Our first few fights were intense, that's for sure. And we can still ratchet up the drama when we want to (we are both "artists," after all). Still, I think we've both come to the realization that life's too short not to choose our battles. We need to take the long view if we're to see our relationships through decades, and being too picky about small issues just isn't worth the fallout.

I need to remind myself that shoes left on the bedroom floor (and in the bathroom, dining room, and living room) aren't that big of a deal. I've heard it many times, and it's true: ask yourself if what you're upset about will matter in five years. If not, step back, pray, and—for the love of all that's holy—choose to be quiet instead of contentious.

What if we made peace with the ways our expectations aren't fulfilled and focused on the positive aspects of our relationship? We could give grace to our spouse and receive the grace they offer.

Soon, instead of claiming that we can't get no satisfaction, we'll want to spend the night together.

Remember: "You Can't Always Get What You Want," so instead of having your "Nineteenth Nervous Breakdown," just "Flip the Switch."

*Lord, sometimes we tend to major on the minors. Forgive us for petty desires, impatient attitudes, and the ways we pick fights with each other. Grant us strength to let little things go, and give us a long-term perspective on marriage.*

## TAKING OFF THE GLOVES

- Talk about what really matters to you in the long run.
- Set a few long-term goals together. Pray about them.
- Why not agree for you each to let one thing go—to not sweat the small stuff?

## TIPS FROM THE PROS

*One of the best things about being married for thirty years is that you can fight for only two minutes before you start laughing at each other. Then next thing you know, you're laughing with each other, and then that's that.*
—KAREN SWALLOW PRIOR, MARRIED 30 YEARS

# BUILDING A "GENERATIONAL" MARRIAGE

*Be good husbands to your wives. Honor them, delight in them. As women they lack some of your advantages. But in the new life of God's grace, you're equals. Treat your wives, then, as equals so your prayers don't run aground.*
1 PETER 3:7 MSG

## SHE SAYS

One day early in our marriage, I visited Carey's office at our church, where he was serving as a youth minister. He was involved in a meeting when I arrived, so I began to joke around with the church receptionist. She mentioned one of Carey's traits that she found challenging in a work environment, and I rolled my eyes. Then I said something downright nasty about him. (I have a sarcastic sense of humor that can get me into trouble.)

Right as I was talking about him in a negative way, Carey walked in, happy to see me. But when he heard my words, his countenance fell. I had hurt his feelings—badly.

I apologized then, and again later, and he graciously forgave me. But that moment—and the look on his face—stuck with me. I vowed to try never to "talk him down" in public or in front of the boys. Joking with my friends about his quirks during girls' night out is sometimes fun, and the Dyers tease each other a lot when we're together. However, putting him down in a mean, snarky way feels like crossing a line.

I want my sons to know that I love and respect their father. Of course I mess up—a lot!—and when I do, I try to own it and apologize to Carey in front of the boys. But for the most part, Carey and I have tried to brag on each other in the presence of our kids, giving each other the honor and respect we deserve.

Someday when Jordan and Jackson are ready to find their spouses, I hope they'll remember parents who were in each other's corner. Then they'll be more likely to find someone who's always in theirs.

## HE SAYS

My dad taught me how to treat a woman. He never sat me down and gave me lessons or anything (awkward). However, my little brain was observing, absorbing, and catching him doing things right.

As of the writing of this book, my folks have been married fifty-two years. In a half century, I'm sure Mom and Dad have had their fair share of mishaps and arguments, but I never once doubted their love for each other. Dad cherishes Mom and vice versa, and if my older brother or I ever got too big for our britches and sassed one of our parents, they were quick to remind our rear ends first (this was before spanking wasn't "in"), and then the rest of us, that their spouse deserved respect. I'm grateful for the lesson.

Even if my parents didn't have a successful marriage, I would still want my relationship with Dena to be "generational." In other words, I want to model for my boys how to honor their future wives—whether that's by looking into Dena's eyes and expressing my love to her, arguing without belittling, or even occasionally dancing in the kitchen like we just don't care. I need to realize that this daily marriage routine doesn't exist just for the two of us. It should also serve as a training ground for the two future hubbies who live with us.

I don't always get it right, and there is something to be said for teaching our sons about God's grace when we goof. But I pray that Dena's and my commitment to each other, as well as Christ's life living through us to honor our vows, serves as relationship seeds that will take root in our kids and bloom into solid marriages down through the years.

*We want to model a healthy marriage, Lord—one that honors You.*
*Help us serve as positive role models for how to treat the opposite sex.*
*Forgive us for the times we serve as negative examples. We are*
*thankful for Your grace and mercy in those times we mess up.*

## TAKING OFF THE GLOVES

- Talk about the term *generational marriage.* Have you ever thought about marriage this way?
- Who modeled a good marriage for you? If they are still around, take time to write them a note or call them and thank them.
- Do you have children? If so, what would you want them to "catch" from the way you treat each other? How could you modify your behavior to prevent them from learning the wrong ways to treat a mate?

## TIPS FROM THE PROS

*He calls me every day before he leaves work to see if I need anything. When he gets home, I ask if I can get him anything. While we don't have a regular date night right now, we do make time together a priority and keep trying new things: a hot air balloon ride, a wine-tasting class, a new music venue. We just keep making more memories together!*
—PAM WATTS, MARRIED 23 YEARS

# TILL DEATH DO US PART

*Then he said to them all: "Whoever wants to be my disciple must deny themselves and take up their cross daily and follow me."*
LUKE 9:23

## HE SAYS

"...till death do us part." As C. S. Lewis simply yet profoundly reminded us, "The pain I feel now is the happiness I had before. That's the deal." One of the trade-offs of sharing your life with someone is knowing that one day you will have to part, briefly separated as one of you slips through earth's boundaries into the eternal. However, I truly believe it's worth it. It's worth hurting that badly if we have gained the privilege of loving so deeply.

Enter Jim and Joan. They met as teenagers in the 1950s, both members of the "luckiest generation." First came love, then came marriage, then came baby in the baby carriage. They didn't begin their faith journey with the Lord until they were almost in their forties, when Jim heard someone talking about Jesus and convinced Joan that they needed to find out more. God's timing was impeccable, because their wedded bliss by this time had crumbled to the brink of divorce. The common bond they found in Christ kept them together for life, and they enjoyed it to the fullest. Adventures abounded as they pursued their need for speed through boating, race cars, and other adventures. Life was good.

As they found their way into their seventies, Jim's bouts of dementia became much more frequent. Joan ended up having to get help for him through the care of a nursing home. And now let me define marriage commitment for you. . . .

Joan visited Jim in that nursing home almost every single day for the last four years of his life: feeding him, taking him outside to feel the sunlight, reading God's Word to him. After a while, he barely recognized her and wasn't even aware of her visits. And although I'm sure that was difficult, it made no difference to her. She had made a commitment decades earlier to stay by his side "till death do us part."

I had the privilege of being a part of Mr. Goodbright's memorial service. Funerals are always sad occasions to some extent. However, on this occasion, I saw on Joan's face the steadiness and peace of a life well-lived—and commitments kept, to the love of her life and to her Lord.

## SHE SAYS

I didn't really think about the "till death" part of our vows at the age of twenty-five. However, we're in our midforties now, and quite a few of our friends and relatives have passed away. And because Carey is on staff at our church, he is asked to sing at many funerals. As we age, the services become more poignant and meaningful.

I pray we both live into our eighties or even nineties, and that we'll deal with life's challenges with grace and humor. If one of us precedes the other in death, I pray that after a suitable mourning period, we'll find companionship and fulfillment with someone like-minded.

But there's another kind of "death" that enduring, faithful marriage entails. It's the kind of death Jesus was referring to when He talked about denying ourselves and taking up our cross daily.

Marriage to a fellow, flawed human being is a laboratory for crucifixion of the flesh. Every day, if we're to follow Christ's example of humility and servanthood, we must set aside our own carnal nature. We put the other person's needs ahead of our own and, as Paul writes in Romans 8:13: "… put to death the deeds of [y]our sinful nature…" The good news? As author Jennifer Kennedy Dean writes, 'Life emerges out of death. The seed that falls into the ground to die to produce a harvest. The branch that is pruned so that it can bear more fruit. The beautiful colors of fall, ushering in the very death that will culminate in the springtime resurrection."[3]

Indeed, every crucifixion is a pathway to resurrection.

*O Lord, we need Your help to put to death the deeds of the flesh. Give us*
*Your strength to put our spouse's needs and concerns above our own.*
*Grant us humility and patience, wisdom and selflessness. Thank You*
*that You didn't leave us alone but gave us the Holy Spirit to help us.*
*Come, Holy Spirit. Bring glorious life out of our "little deaths."*

## TAKING OFF THE GLOVES

- Talk about a couple you both know in which one spouse has outlived the other. How did the surviving spouse cope? Pray for that widow or widower together.
- Have you ever thought about marriage as a laboratory for crucifixion of the flesh? What does that mean to you?

---

3. http://www.prayinglife.org/2012/10/an-altard-state/

- How could you die to yourself daily in your marriage? Ask the Holy Spirit for creative ways to unselfishly serve your spouse.

## TIPS FROM THE PROS

*If we've argued, I never go to bed or leave the house without apologizing, no matter if I feel that I'm right (which I usually do!). I fear that it might be our last conversation, and I don't want to regret not saying I love you. That would be worse than losing the argument.*

—Merna Lewis, married 9 years

# NOTES

# NOTES

# NOTES

# RECOMMENDED RESOURCES

## MINISTRIES

Family Life Ministries
Focus on the Family
Life Recovered (especially for ministry couples)
Marriage Builders
Marriage Today
New Life Ministries


## AUTHORS/SPEAKERS

Steve Arterburn
Gary Chapman
Crown Financial Resources
John and Stasi Eldredge
Pam and Bill Farrel
Shaunti and Jeff Feldhan
Sheila Wray Gregoire
Jay and Laura Laffoon
Steve McVey
Les and Leslie Parrott
Dennis and Barbara Rainey
Dave Ramsey
Anita and John Renfroe
Gary Smalley
Gary Thomas
John Townsend and Henry Cloud
Fawn Weaver, The Happy Wives Club
H. Norman Wright

**AUTHOR BIOS**

# ABOUT THE AUTHORS

**Carey Dyer** can often be found watching an episode of *The Andy Griffith Show* and/or drinking a Mountain Dew. Before his call to full-time ministry, Carey logged thousands of hours on stage as a professional entertainer— even dancing around in a grass skirt with a rubber chicken on a stick (no, really, they paid him and everything).

After years in the spotlight, Carey sensed God's call to express his talents in a different way. Now, when he's not leading worship in his church, he enjoys traveling to other churches, banquets, and conferences and ministering through his unique bag of tricks. Carey is also a published scriptwriter, choral arranger/composer, and essay writer.

**Dena Dyer**'s busy days are often fueled by coffee and dark chocolate. As a second grader, she began composing short stories and discovered a passion that became a calling. Her résumé includes jobs such as public relations news writer, communications director, professional music theater actress, and drama teacher.

Currently, Dena is a professional speaker, writer, and teacher whose articles and tips have appeared in dozens of magazines, such as *Family Circle*, *Redbook*, *Writer's Digest*, *Home Life*, *Focus on the Family*, and *Reader's Digest*. Dena has written four books (*Grace for the Race: Meditations for Busy Moms*, *Mothers of the Bible*, *Let the Crow's Feet and Laugh Lines Come*, and *25 Christmas Blessings*) and coauthored four others, including *Wounded Women of the Bible: Finding Hope When Life Hurts* with Tina Samples.

Carey and Dena have been married for twenty years and have two sons, Jordan and Jackson. The Dyers make their home about forty-five minutes southwest of Fort Worth in Granbury, Texas—which is big enough to have a Walmart but not an Olive Garden. To find out more about their separate or combined ministries, visit careyanddena.com.

# SCRIPTURE INDEX

# IF YOU LIKED THIS BOOK, YOU'LL ALSO LIKE...

*Jehova-Rapha: The God Who Heals*
by Mary J. Nelson
*Jehovah-Rapha: The God Who Heals* features 72 comforting and encouraging meditations and stories based on healing scriptures—pointing readers to God, the Ultimate Healer. Written by author, speaker, pastor of prayer, and cancer survivor, Mary J. Nelson shares the Word without compromise, releases hope, and focuses on the heavenly Father's infinite love and grace.
Paperback / 978-1-63409-198-5 / $14.99

*Dangerous Prayer*
by Cheri Fuller
Join gifted speaker and award-winning author, Cheri Fuller, as she illustrates—from Bible times to today—what happens when God's people pray dangerous prayers. Each of the 21 chapters is rooted in scripture and weaves together a beautiful tapestry of lives and kingdoms impacted through the power of prayer.
Paperback / 978-1-63409-115-2 / $14.99